TONY HARRISON

The Mysteries

faber and faber
LONDON · BOSTON

This collection first published 1985
by Faber and Faber Limited
3 Queen Square London WC1N 3AU
Reprinted 1986, 1988 and 1990

Printed in Great Britain by
Richard Clay Ltd Bungay Suffolk

British Library Cataloguing in Publication Data

Harrison, Tony, *1937–*
The mysteries.
I. Title
822'.914   PR6058.A69435
ISBN 0–571–13789–X
ISBN 0–571–13790–3 Pbk

CONTENTS

The process by which the Mystery Plays were originally created has been described as 'one of translation, accretion, adaptation, revision'. It was in a similar fashion that I worked with the Cottesloe Company, offering myself as a Yorkshire poet who came to read the metre and to monitor the preservation of the plays' Northern character. During my absence in America other members of the Company also worked on the text, notably John Russell Brown, Bill Bryden and Jack Shepherd, especially in *The Nativity* production of 1980. Some of that work was revised to give the final dramatic shape to the three-part final production of *The Mysteries* and to fashion this text.

TH
National Theatre
May 1985

From the first performance of *The Passion* on Easter Saturday 1977, on the terraces of the National Theatre, to the re-opening of the entire trilogy at the Lyceum Theatre, 18 May 1985, the Company has included:

Peter Armitage	Caroline Hutchison
Alun Armstrong	Kenny Ireland
John Barrett	Philip Jackson
Brenda Blethyn	Olu Jacobs
Timothy Block	Karl Johnson
Dai Bradley	Richard Johnson
Gil Brailey	Maya Kemp
David Busby	Dave King
Peter Carlisle	Philip Langham
Jim Carter	Alfred Lynch
Jeffrey Chiswick	Eve Matheson
Oliver Cotton	Fulton Mackay
Kenneth Cranham	Mark McManus
J. G. Devlin	Kevin McNally
Philip Donaghy	Mary Miller
Edna Dore	Paul Moriarty
Ken Drury	Derek Newark
Lynn Farleigh	Robert Oates
Albert Finney	Bill Owen
Ann Firbank	Stephen Petcher
Barry Foster	Clarke Peters
Christoper Gilbert	John Price
Brian Glover	Bryan Pringle
Michael Gough	Trevor Ray
Howard Goorney	David Roper
Glyn Grain	Barrie Rutter
Gawn Grainger	John Salthouse
James Grant	Jack Shepherd
Tony Haygarth	Keith Skinner
Paul Henley	Dinah Stabb
Greg Hicks	Robert Stephens
Dave Hill	John Tams

Trevor Thomas
Derek Thompson
Anthony Trent
Frederick Treves
Frederick Warder
Don Warrington

June Watson
Valerie Whittington
Pitt Wilkinson
Tom Wilkinson
Paul Young

The first performance of the entire trilogy was in the Cottesloe Theatre on 19 January 1985

Director   Bill Bryden
Designer   William Dudley
Lighting   William Dudley & Laurence Clayton
Music Director   John Tams
Music   arranged and performed by The Home Service
Dances   arranged by David Busby
Staff Director   Frank Nealon
Production Manager   Jason Barnes
Asst. to Bill Bryden   John Caulfield
Deputy Stage Manager   Trish Montemuro
Asst. Stage Managers   Peter Maccoy, Jane Suffling
Sound   Chris Montgomery

THE NATIVITY

CHARACTERS

GOD
ANGEL LUCIFER (SATAN)
ANGEL GABRIEL
ADAM
EVE
ANGEL
BOY
ABEL
CAIN
NOAH
WIFE
ABRAHAM
ISAAC
JOSEPH
MARY
HEROD
MESSENGER
SON
THREE KINGS
THREE SHEPHERDS
MAK
MAK'S WIFE
TWO SOLDIERS
TWO WOMEN
KNIGHT
HERALD
DEATH

The COMPANY *in the various uniforms and overalls of carpenter, painter, butcher, fireman, bus conductor, ticket collector, fishmonger, miner, mechanic, meat-porter, cleaner, gas fitter, construction worker, etc., greet the audience as they arrive and talk with them. The leader of the* BAND *welcomes the audience to the first part of the* THE MYSTERIES *and the* BAND *begins a polka tune. The* COMPANY *dances to the tune, and the audience are invited to clap along.*
After the music GOD *enters on a fork-lift truck.*

Fanfare

GOD

Ego sum alpha et omega,
Vita, via, veritas
Primus et novissimus.

(Fanfare)

I am gracious and great, God withouten beginning;
I am maker unmade, all might is in me.
I am life and way unto wealth winning;
I am foremost and first; als I bid shall it be.
My blessing in bliss shall be blending,
And harboured from harm, shall be hidden;
My body in bliss aye abiding,
Enduring without any ending.

(As GOD *speaks* LUCIFER *enters and stands on a black box.* ANGEL GABRIEL *stands on the second level facing* GOD.*)*

Since I am maker unmade, and most high in might,
And aye shall be endless, and nought is but I,
Unto my dignity dear shall duly be dight
A bliss all-abundant about me.
In the which bliss I bid that be here
Nine orders of angels full clear,
In loving aye lasting to lout me.

(to LUCIFER)

> Thee, mightiest of all I made, most after me;
> I make thee as master and mirror of my might;
> I set thee here by me in bliss for to be,
> And name thee for Lucifer, als bearer of light.

ANGEL LUCIFER

> All the mirth that is made is markèd in me.
> The beams of my brighthood are burning so bright,
> And so seemly in sight myself I now see.
> Like a lord am I lifted to live in this light:

(LUCIFER *is lifted by members of the* COMPANY *off his platform and carried to his 'throne', an armchair placed on a fork-lift truck.)*

> More fairer than friends it appears;
> In me is no point to impair.
> I feel me well favoured and fair;
> My power is passing my peers.

ANGEL GABRIEL

> Lord, with a lasting love we laud thee alone,
> You mightiful maker that marked us and made us,
> And wrought us thus worthely to dwell as thy own
> Where never feeling of filth may foul us nor fade us.
> All bliss is abundant about us,
> The while we are stable in thought
> In the worship of him that us wrought;
> Of dread need we never more doubt us.

ANGEL LUCIFER

> Oh what!
> I am favoured and fair and figured full fit;
> The form of all fairhood upon me is fast.
> All wealth in my wield is, I wete by my wit;
> The beams of my brighthood are bigged with the best.
> My showing is shimmering and shining,
> So bigly to bliss am I brought;
> Me needs for to 'noy me right nought;
> Here shall never pain bring me pining.

12

ANGEL GABRIEL

With all the wit that we wield we worship thy will,
Thou glorious God that is ground of all grace:
Aye with steadfast sound let us stand still,
Lord! to be fed with the food of thy fair face.
In life that is loyal aye-lasting,
Thy dole, Lord, is aye daintethly dealing;
And whoso that food may be feeling,
To see thy fair face, is not fasting.

ANGEL LUCIFER

Ow! Certes! What!
Me beseemeth my beams they are brighter than
bright!
Magnificent, mighty, am I, by Mahowne!
In heaven shall I set myself, full seemly to sight,
To receive my reverence through right of renown.
I shall be like unto him that is highest on height!
Oh what! I am worthy and wise . . .

(LUCIFER'S *chair begins to descend.*)

Out! Deuce! All goes down.
My beams ere so shining all beshitten and shent
I fall to fierce fire through t'whole firmament.
From heaven I am hurled down on all hand
Help! Harrow! Helpless!

(LUCIFER *sees a smoking cauldron beneath him.*)

So hot is it here!
Never was space ere so speedily spanned!
This is a dungeon of dole in which I am dight.
Where is my kindred so comely and clear?
Now am I laithliest, alas, that ere was so light,
My brightness, Beelzebub, blackest and blue now.
My bale is ay beating and burning
That gars me go growling and girning.
Out, Ribald, wracked am I by rue now.

13

Thrust into this fire, flung out for a thought!
So speedily spilled no sooner I'd spoke.

(LUCIFER *leaps into a smoking cauldron manned by two of the*
COMPANY *we will later see play* RIBALD *and* BEELZEBUB.)

I wist not this woe should be wrought
Out on ye, lurdans, ye smore me in smoke.

(*The two men spin the cauldron through the audience as the* BAND
plays 'Lucifer's Song'.)

Pride is out and pride is in
Pride is root of every sin
Pride will always fight to win
Til he has brought a man to woe.

Man beware or fall in woe
Consider pride and let it go.

Lucifer was angel bright
A conqueror of power and might
But through his pride he lost his sight
And fell to everlasting woe.

Man beware or fall in woe
Consider pride and let it go.

GOD

These fools from their fair-hood in fantasies fell;
They would not me worship that wrought them.
Wherefore shall my wrath e'er go with them.
And all that me worship shall dwell here, I wis.
Since earth is vain void and in murkness doth dwell,
I bid in my blessing the angels give light.
The murkness thus name I for 'night',
The 'day' do I call this clear light.
A firmament I bid appear;
And that same shall be named heaven,
With planets and with cloud full clear.

14

The sun and moon in fair manner
Now greatly gang in your degree;
For ye shall set the seasons here,
Day from day and year from year.
The water I will be here
To flow both far and near,
The largest part I name the 'sea',
Gathering of waters clear.
And with the sea I will begin.
Whales all quick in sea will dwell,
And other fish to flit with fin,
Some with scale and some with shell.
The land shall foster and forth bring
Buxsomly by me decreed
Herbs and fruit to fill and feed,
Trees also thereon shall spring,
And flowers fair on height to hang,
And winging with the wind on high
I bid be fowls full fair to fly.
All divers beasts on land I send,
To breed and be with bale forth brought;
And with the beasts I will to blend
Serpents to be seen unsought,
And worms upon their wombs will wend
To woe in earth and worth to nought.
And so it shall be kenned
How all is made that ought;
Beginning, midd'st and end
I with my word have wrought.

(Maypole dance represents the Creation. ADAM *and* EVE *appear.)*

To keep this world both more and less
A skilful beast then will I make
After my shape and my likeness,
The which shall worship to me take.
Of the simplest part of earth that is here
I shall make man.

Rise up, thou earth, in blood and bone,
In shape of man, I command thee.

(ADAM *rises.*)

A female shalt thou have to feere –
Here shall I make of thy left rib.

(EVE *rises.*)

She alone shall be thy dear
To keep thee warm, through night in t'crib.
Take now here the ghost of life,
And receive both your souls of me.
This female take thou to thy wife:
Adam, and Eve, your names shall be.

Adam and Eve, this is the place
That I have grant you of my grace
To have your dwelling in.
Herbs, spice, fruit on tree,
Beasts, fowls, all that ye see,
Shall bow to you therein.
This place hight Paradise;
Here shall your joys begin.

ADAM

O Lord! loved be thy name.
For now is this a joyful home
For thou has brought us to,
Full of solace, calm and mirth,
Herbs and trees and fruit on earth,
With spices many too.
Lo, Eve, now are we brought
Both unto rest and roo.
We need to take no thought,
But look all well to do.

EVE

Loving be aye to such a lord
To us has given so great reward,
To govern both great and small,
And made us after his own mind
Such pleasure and such play to find
Amongst these mirths all.
Here is a joyful sight
Where we in peace shall dwell.
We love thee, most of might,
Great God, perpetual.

GOD

Love my name with good intent
And hark to my commandment;
My bidding both obey.
Of all the fruit in Paradise
Take ye thereof in your best wise,
And make you right merry.
The tree of good and ill –
What time you eat of this,
Thou speeds thyself to spill,
And be brought out of bliss.

ADAM

Alas, Lord, that we should do so ill.
Thy blessed bidding we shall fulfil,
Both in thought and in deed.
We shall not nigh this tree nor bough,
Nor yet the fruit that on it grow,
Therewith our flesh to feed.

EVE

We shall do thy bidding;
We have no other need.
The fruit full still shall hang,
Lord, that thou hast forbid.

GOD

Here shall you lead your life
With dainties that is dear.
Adam, and Eve thy wife,
My blessing have you here.

(GOD *and* ANGEL *exeunt.* SATAN *appears in smoking cauldron.*)

SATAN

Alas, my wits are wode with woe!
Ah Lucifer, why fell thou so?
I, that was an angel fair
And sat so high above the air,
Now am I waxen black as coal,
And ugly, tattered as a fool.
What ailed thee, Lucifer, to fall?
Was thou not fairest of angels all?
Brightest and best, and most of love
With God himself that sits above.
Alas the joy that I was in
Have I lost through my sin.
But hearken all what I shall say
That joy that I have lost for ay
God has made man with his hand
To have that bliss withouten end.
If I myself am barred from bliss
I shall make man do much amiss.
I, Lucifer, exiled from light
Shall the bliss of mankind blight.
By Mahowne, I'll mar for ay
The cleanness of God's lump of clay.
To Adam's mate I will me hie.
In a worm-likeness will I wend.
And feign for her a likely lie.
Eve! Eve!

EVE

Who is there?

SATAN

I, a friend.

(A snake is formed by the COMPANY *linking hands with* SATAN. *They dance)*

Of all the fruit that ye see hang
In Paradise, which eat ye not?

EVE

We may of them ilka one
Take all that us good thought;
Save one tree out is ta'en,
Would do harm to nigh it aught.

SATAN

And why that tree – That would I wit
Any more than all other by?

EVE

For our Lord God forbids us it,
The fruit thereof, Adam nor I,
To nigh it near;
And if we did, we both should die,
He said, and cease our solace here.

SATAN

Ah, Eve, to me tak tent;
Tak heed, and thou shalt hear
What that same matter meant
He moved on thus my dear.
To eat thereof he you forfend –
I know it well; this was his skill –
Because he would none other kenned
Those great virtues that longs there still.
For wilt thou see?
Who eats the fruit of good and ill
Shall have knowing as well as he.

EVE

Why, what kin' thing art thou,
That tells this tale to me?

SATAN

A worm, that wots well how
That ye may worshipped be.

EVE

What worship should we win thereby
To eat thereof as needs it not?
We have lordship to make mastery
Of all things that in earth are wrought.

SATAN

Woman, do way!
To greater state ye may be brought,
If ye will do as I shall say.

EVE

To do is us full loath
That should our God mispay.

SATAN

Nay, certes, no harm for both;
Eat it safely ye may.
For peril, right there none in lies,
But worship and a great winning;
For right as God ye shall be wise,
And peer to him in all kin' thing.
Ay, gods shall ye be,
Of ill and good to have knowing,
For to be als wise as he.

EVE

Is this sooth that thou says?

SATAN

Yea; why trust thou not me?
I would by no kind ways
Tell nought but truth to thee.

20

EVE

Then will I to thy teaching trust,
And take this fruit unto our food.

SATAN

Bit on boldly; be not abashed.
And give Adam to amend his mood
And eke his bliss.

(She bites. SATAN *laughs.)*

EVE

Adam, have here of fruit full good.

ADAM

Alas, woman! Why took thou this?
Our Lord commanded us both
To tend this tree of his.
Thy work will make him wroth;
Alas, thou has done amiss.

EVE

Nay, Adam, grieve thee nought at it,
And I shall say the reason why.
A worm has done me for to wit
We shall be as gods, thou and I,
If that we eat
Here of this tree. Adam, thereby
Let not that worship for to get.
For we shall be as wise
As God that is so great,
And als mickle of price;
Therefore eat of this meat.

ADAM

To eat it would I not eschew,
Might I me sure in thy saying.

EVE

Bite on boldly, for it is true,
We shall be gods, and know all things.

ADAM

To win that name
I shall it taste at thy teaching.

(Bites. SATAN laughs.)

Alas! What have I done? For shame!
Ill counsel! Woe worth thee!
Ah, Eve, thou art to blame;
To this enticed thou me.
My body does me shame,
For I am naked, as me think.

EVE

Alas, Adam, right so am I.

ADAM

And for sorrow sore why might we not sink?
For we have grieved God almighty
That made me man;
Broken his bidding bitterly –
Alas, that ever we began!
This work, Eve, hast thou wrought,
And made this bad bargain.

EVE

Nay, Adam; blame me not.

ADAM

Do way, love Eve; who then?

EVE

The worm to wite well worthy were,
With tales untrue he me betrayed.

ADAM

Alas, that I list to thy lore,
Or trusted the trifles that thou me said;
So may I bide.
For I may ban that bitter braid
And dreary deed that I it did.

Our shape for dole me grieves.
Wherewith shall they be hid?

EVE

Let us take these fig leaves,
Since it is thus betide.

ADAM

Right as thou says, so shall it be,
For we are naked and all bare.
Full wonder fain I would hide me
From my Lord's sight, if I wist where –
Where I not care.

(GOD *appears*.)

GOD

Adam! Adam!

ADAM

Lord!

GOD

Where art thou, there?

ADAM

I hear thee, Lord, and see thee not.

GOD

Say, whereto does it belong,
This work? Why hast thou wrought?

ADAM

Lord, Eve made me do wrong,
And to this breach has brought.

GOD

Say, Eve, why hast thou made thy mate
Eat fruit I bade thee should hang still,
And commanded none of it to take?

EVE

A worm, Lord, enticed me theretill.
So welaway!
That ever I did that deed so ill!

GOD

Ah, wicked worm! Woe worth thee aye!
For thou on this manner
Has made them such affray.
My malison have thou here,
With all the might I may.
And on thy womb then shalt thou glide,
And be aye full of enmity.
To all mankind on ilka side;
And earth it shall thy sustance be
To eat and drink.
Adam and Eve, also ye
In earth then shall ye sweat and swink
And travail for your food.

ADAM

Alas, when might we sink,
We that has all world's good?
Full grievous may us think.

GOD

Now Cherubim, mine angel bright,
To middle earth tight go drive these two.

ANGEL

All ready, Lord, as it is right,
Since thy will is that it be so
And thy liking.
Adam and Eve, do you two go,
For here may ye make no dwelling.
Go ye forth fast, to fare;
Of sorrow may ye sing.

ADAM

Alas, for shame and sorrow sad.
Mourning makes me mazed and mad;
To think in heart what help I had,
And now has none;
On ground may I never go glad;
My games are gone.
Gone are my games wi'outen glee.
Alas, in bliss couth we not be?
For put we were to great plenty
At prime o' day.
By time of noon all lost had we.
So welaway!

The Killing of Abel

Enter BOY, *with five horses.*

BOY

Make room, make room for Adam's kin
Are coming here for t'worshippin' –
T'Ploughman Cain and Shepherd Abel
Brothers both as told in't fable
With five fine fillies, plough and pack.
They laboured long with bended back.
Tak tent, 'tis truth I tell to thee:
So stand stock still and ye shall see.

(*Music:* CAIN *enters ploughing.*
Horse dance.
ABEL *enters with a sheep.*)

ABEL

God, as he both may and can,
Speed thee, brother, and thy man.

CAIN

Come kiss mine arse! I will not ban:
But away from here is your welcome.

25

Thou should ha' stayed till thou were called.
Come near and either drive or hold,
And kiss the devil's bum.
Go graze thy sheep, under and out,
For that to thee is lief.

ABEL

Brother, there is none about
To wish thee any grief.

But, brother dear, hear my saw:
It is the custom of our law,
That all the workers that are wise
Shall worship God with sacrifice.

Come forth, brother, and let us gang
To worship God: we stay too long.

CAIN

Should I leave my plough and everything
And go with thee to make off'ring?
Nay, thou findst me not so mad.
Go to the devil, and say I bad!
What gives God to thee, to praise him so?
He gives me nought but sorrow and woe.

ABEL

Cain, leave this vain carping.
For God gives thee thy living.

CAIN

Borrowed I never yet a farthing
Of him! – Here is my hand!

ABEL

Brother, as our elders gave command,
A tithe should we offer with our hand,
A tenth of our goods to be burnt with the brand.

(ABEL *with a sheep and* CAIN *with a stook of corn prepare
sacrifice.*)

CAIN

Lay down thy bundle upon this hill.

ABEL

Forsooth, brother, so I will.
And God of heaven, take it for good.

CAIN

Now offer first thy livelihood.

ABEL

God that shaped both earth and sky
I pray to thee, thou hear my cry:
Now take with thanks, if thy will be,
The tithe that I offer here to thee;
For I give it with good intent
To thee, my Lord, that all has sent.
I burn it now with steadfast thought,
In worship of him that all has wrought.

(White smoke appears.)

CAIN

Against my will is it, full sorely,
The tithe that I here give to thee,
Of corn and things that grow for me.
But I'll begin since it's my turn
And I must needs my tenth to burn.
One sheaf, *one;* and this makes two!

(He begins to count the sheaves, holding back the best for himself.)

Yet neither can I spare for you.
Two, two; now this is three: –
Yea, this also shall stay with me,
For I will choose the best to have.
This is thy due – of all, this sheaf.
At last! At last! Four! Lo, here!

(He has chosen a very small ragged sheaf.)

Better grew I none this year.
At spring-time I sowed fair corn,
Yet was it such when it was shorn:
Thistles and briers – yea, great plenty! –
And all kind of weeds that might be.
Four sheaves, four. Lo, this makes five –
If I deal out thus, I'll never thrive! –
Five, and six; now this is seven –
But this goes never to God in heaven;
Nor none of these four from my right
Shall ever come into God's sight.
Seven . . . seven. Now this is eight.

ABEL

Cain, brother, you call on God's hate.

CAIN

Nine, ten; and two more,
There now is all my store,
Whee! Fire! Help me! Help to blow!
It will not burn for me, I trow.
Puff! This smoke does me much shame –
Now, burn, in the devil's name!

(Black smoke appears.)

Ah! What devil of hell is it?
My lungs almost had been split.
Had I blown then one blast more
I had been choked right sore.
It stank like the devil in hell,
So longer there might I not dwell.

ABEL

Cain, this is not worth one leek;
Thy tithe should burn without this stink.

CAIN

Come kiss the devil right in the arse;
Because of *thee* it burns the worse.

I would that it were in thy throat,
Fire and sheaf, and every sprout.

(GOD *appears above.*)

GOD

Cain, why art thou such a rebel
Against thy brother, Abel?
To flite and chide there is no need.
If thou tithe right, thou getst thy meed;
And be thou sure, if thou tithe false,
Thou shall be paid with nothing else.

(GOD *withdraws.*)

CAIN

Why, who is that hob-over-the-wall?
Whee! Who was that that piped so small?
Come go we hence from perils all:
God is out of his wit.
Come forth, Abel, and let us wend.
Methink that God is not my friend;
Away, then, must I flit.

ABEL

Ah, Cain, brother, that is ill done.
God's will I trow it were
That mine did burn so clear.

CAIN

Why, yea! And thou for that shall pay!
With cheek-bone, ere my hand I stay,
Shall I have torn thy life away.

(CAIN *strikes* ABEL *with a cheek-bone.*)

So lie down there and take thy rest;
Thus loud-mouths are chastised best.

ABEL

Vengeance, vengeance, Lord, I cry!
For I am slain, and not guilty.

(ABEL dies. GOD appears above.)

GOD

Cain! Cain!

CAIN

Who is that that calls me?
I am here, mayest thou not see?

GOD

Cain, where is thy brother Abel?

CAIN

Why ask of me? I think in hell;
In hell I think he be.
Whoso were there, might him see.
Or somewhere he may be sleeping;
When was he in my keeping?

GOD

Cain, Cain, thou art wild and mad:
The voice of thy brother's blood
That thou has slain in false wise,
From earth to heaven on vengeance cries.
And, for thou has brought thy brother down
Here I give thee malediction,
I mark thee Cain. This for thy bane:
Forever plead for death, in vain,
Lest ye be damned, all him disdain.

(An ANGEL marks CAIN. GOD withdraws.)

CAIN

No matter! I wot whither I shall:
In hell, I wot, must be my stall.
It is no use mercy to crave;
For if I pray, none must I have.

Farewell. When I am dead
Bury me in Wakefield by t'quarry head.
Damned for my deed I now depart.
By all men set I not a fart.

(Drags body off stage. Exit.
Song: 'Cain and Abel'.)

BAND

Don't be an outlaw
Don't be so wayward
Having your own way
When you could be a friend to me
Working together
That's what's meant to happen
Planning a new day
Will you give your hand to me.

I can be mindless as a bird
If I've a mind to be
I can be free.
Bowing to no one in the world
Leaving it up to me
I can be free.

(Words and music: Bill Caddick. Published by Highway Music.)

(Enter NOAH.*)*

NOAH

Sin is now abroad,   without any repentance.
Six hundred years and odd   have I, without distance,
On earth, as any sod,   lived with great grievance
    Alway;
And now I wax old,
Sick, sorry and cold;
As muck upon mould
    I widder away.

*(*NOAH *kneels.)*

But yet will I cry   for mercy, and call.
Noah, thy servant, am I,   Lord over all!
Therefore me – and my fry   that shall with me fall –
Save from villainy,   and bring to thy hall
    In heaven

And keep me from sin
This world within.

Comely King of Mankind,
    I pray thee hear my saying.

(GOD *appears from above.*)

            GOD

I repent full sore   that ever made I man;
By me he sets no store,   and I am his sovereign.
I will destroy therefore   both beast, man and woman:
All shall perish, less and more.   Their bargain may
                         they ban
    That ill did do.
On earth I see right nought
But sin that is unsought;
Of those that well ha' wrought
    Find I but a few.

Therefore shall I fordo   all this middle-world
With floods that shall flow   and roar hideous abroad.
I have good cause thereto;   of me no man's afeard.
As I say, so shall I do: for vengeance draw my sword,
    And make end
Of all that bear a life,
Save Noah and his wife,
For they would never strife
    With me, nor me offend.

(GOD *descends to address* NOAH.)

    Noah, my friend, I thee command,   from sorrows thee
                        to shield
    A ship that thou should frame   of nail and board full
                        well.
    Thou alway was a good workman,   to me as true as
                        steel,
    To my bidding obedient;   friendship shall thou feel
    As thy reward.

In length thy ship should be
Three hundred cubits, warn I thee;
In height even thirty,
 Of fifty also broad.

NOAH

Ah! Benedicite! What art thou that thus
Tells me before that which shall be? Thou art full
          marvellous;
Tell me, for charity, thy name so gracious.

GOD

My name is of dignity, and also full glorious
 To know:
I am God most mighty
One God, in Trinity,
Made thee and ev'ry man to be;
 To love me well thou owe.

(NOAH *falls to his knees.*)

Noah, to thee and to thy fry
My blessing grant I;
Ye shall wax and multiply
 And fill the earth again,

When all these floods are past and fully gone away.

(*Exit* GOD.)

NOAH

Lord, homeward will I haste as fast as that I may;
My wife will I ask what she wills to say;
And I am aghast that we get some fray
 Betwixt us both,
For she bites sharply;
For little's oft angry.
If anything wrong be,
 Soon is she wroth.

(*He now speaks to his* WIFE.)

God speed, dear wife!   How fare ye?

WIFE

Now, as ever might I thrive,   the worse that I thee see.
Do tell me in brief   where has thou thus long be?
To death may we drive,   for all it means to thee,
  For want.
When we sweat and swynk,
Thou does just as thou think;
Yet of meat and of drink
  Have we real skant.

NOAH

Wife, we are hard stead   with tidings anew.

WIFE

But thou were worthy be clad   in black and blue,
For that art alway afraid,   be it false or true.
But God knows that I am treated   – and that may I rue
  Full ill;
I trust from thee may borrow,
From evening until morrow
Thou speakst ever of sorrow.
  God send thee once thy fill.

(She addresses women in the audience.)

We women must harry   all ill husbands.
I have one by Mary   that loosed me from my bands!
If he be troubled, I must tarry   – howsoever it stands –
With semblance full sorry,   and wring both my hands
  For fear;
But still, otherwhile,
What with game and with guile,
I shall smite and smile,
  And pay him back dear.

NOAH

Whey! Hold thy tongue, ram-skyte,   or I shall
  thee still.

WIFE

By my shrift, if thou smite,   turn on thee I will.

NOAH

We shall assay ye as tight.   Have at thee, Gill!
Upon the bone shall it bite.

(He strikes her.)

WIFE

Ah, so! Mary, thou smitest ill
    But I suppose
I shall not in thy debt
From this floor now flit:
Take thee there a langett
    To tie up thy hose!

(She strikes him.)

NOAH

Ah! Wilt thou so?   Mary, that is mine!

WIFE

Thou shall ha' three for two,   I swear by God's pain!

NOAH

And I shall quite thee then though in faith or in sin.

WIFE

Out upon thee, ho!

NOAH

Thou can both bite and whine;
And thou roared.

(He turns to audience.)

For all if she strike
She will furious skrike;
In faith, I hold none her like
    In all middle-world.

But I will keep charity,   for I have much to do.

WIFE

Here shall no man tarry thee;   I pray thee to go!
Full well may we miss thee,   as ever have I rue.
To spin will I set me.

(She sits down to spin.)

NOAH

Whey! farewell, lo!
But wife,
Pray for me busily,
Till after I come to thee.

WIFE

Even as thou pray'st for me,
As ever might I thrive.

NOAH

I tarry full long   from my work, I trow;
Now my gear will I bring   and thitherward draw.

(He goes to build his ship. The keel is brought on.)

Now assay will I
What I know of shipwrightry
In nomine Patris, et Fillii,
Et Spiritus Sancti.   Amen.

To begin with this tree   my bones will I bend;
I trust that the Trinity   succour will send.

(SHIPWRIGHTS enter. The Ark is built. NOAH speaks from the Ark.)

Wife, have done; come into ship fast.

WIFE

(Spinning)

Aye, Noah, go clout thy shoon!   The better will they
last.

NOAH

Now is this twice come in,   dame, on my friendship.

WIFE

Whether I lose or I win,   in faith, thy fellowship,
Set I not at a pin.   This spindle will I slip
    Upon this hill
Ere I stir once a foot.

NOAH

Peter!   I trow that we dote.
Without any more note,
    Come in if ye will.

WIFE

Aye, the water nighs so near   that I sit not dry;
Into ship with a fleer,   therefore, will I hie
For dread that I drown here.

(She hurries to the Ark. Then she turns to women in the audience.)

Lord, I were at ease,   and in heart quite whole,
Might I once have a mess   of widow's cawl.
For *thy* soul, without lies,   should I deal penny dole:
So would more, and no fuss,   that I see in this hall
    Among wives that are here,
For the life that they lead
Wish their husbands were dead;
For, as ever eat I bread,
    So wish I our sire were!

(NOAH turns to the men in the audience.)

NOAH

Ye men that have wives,   whiles they are young,
If ye love your own lives,   chastise their tongue.
Methink my heart rives   – and both liver and lung –
To see such-like strifes   wedded men among.

(NOAH goes to steer the Ark.)

Now to the helm will I hent,
And to my ship attend.

WIFE

I see in the firmament,
    Methinks, the seven stars.

NOAH

This is a great flood,   wife, take heed.

WIFE

So methought, as I stood.   We are in great dread;
These waves are so wode.

NOAH

              Help, God, in this need!
As thou art steersman good,   and the best, as I rede,
    Of all,
Thou rule us in this race,
As thou did me promise.

WIFE

This is a perilous case.
    Help, God, when we call!

(Song: 'When my Ship comes in'.)

BAND

Oh the time will come up.
When the winds will stop.
And the seas will cease to be a breathing,
Like the stillness in the wind,
Before the hurricane begins,
The hour that our ship comes in.
Then the sands will roll out a carpet of gold.
For your weary toes to be a touching
And the ship's wise men will remind you once again
That the whole wide world is watching.

(Words and music: Bob Dylan)

NOAH

This forty days has rain been;   it will therefore abate,

As God did reveal.
Now am I aghast –
It is waned a great deal!

Now are the weathers ceased,   and cateracts up-knit,
Both the most and the least.

WIFE

Methink, by my wit,
The sun shines in the east.   Lo, is not yond it?
We should have a good feast,   where these floods flit
So spitous.

NOAH

We have been here, all we,
Three hundred days and fifty.
Aye, now wains the sea;
Lord, well is us.

WIFE

What ground may this be?

NOAH

The hills of Armenie.

Dame, therefore thy counsel me,   what fowl best
might
Know how
With flight of its wing,
To bring without tarrying,
Of mercy some tokening,
Either from north or from south.

(The dove flies off. Music.)

Now this is the first day   of the tenth moon.

WIFE

Hence in just a little,   she is coming: lew! lew!

(Dove returns. Music.)

She is bringing in her bill   some tidings new
    Behold!
It is of an olive-tree
A branch, it seems to me.

NOAH

It is sooth, perdy;
    Right so is it called

Dove, bird fully blest,   fair may thee befall!
Thou art true to thy tryst,   as stone in the wall.
Full well I it wist   thou'd come back to thy hall.

WIFE

A true token is't   we shall be saved all.
    For why?
The water, since she come
Of deepness to plumb
Is fallen a fathom
    And more certainly.

(They leave the Ark. Music.)

But Noah, where are now all our kin
And company we knew before?

NOAH

Dame, all are drowned.   Let be thy din,
For soon they bought their sins full sore.
Good living let us now begin
So that we grieve our God no more.
He set his bow clearly to ken
As a token betwixt him and us,
For knowledge to all Christian men,
That since this world was finished thus
With water would be ne'er waste again.
Thus has God most of might
Set up his sign full clear,
Up in the air in height;
The rainbow it is right,

40

As men may see in sight,
In seasons of the year.

(ISAAC *runs on and* ABRAHAM *follows with rabbit snares.*
ABRAHAM *kneels.)*

ABRAHAM

Abraham I am namèd
And patriarch of age full old
And yet by the grace of God is bred
In mine old age a child full bold,
Isaac lo his name is told
My sweet son that standeth me by.
Among all children that walk on wold
A lovelier child is none truly.

I thank God with heart full mild
Of his great mercy and his high grace
And principally for my sweet child
That shall to me do great solace.
Now sweet son, so fair of face
Full heartily do I love thee.
For true hearty love now in this place
My sweet child come kiss now me.

ISAAC

At your bidding your mouth I kiss
With lowly heart I you pray
Your fatherly love let me never miss
But bless me, your child, both night and day.

ABRAHAM

There may no man love better his child
Than Isaac here is loved of me
Almighty God merciful and mild
For my sweet son I worship thee
I thank thee Lord with heart full free
For this fair fruit thou hast me sent
Now gracious God where so he be
To save my son ever more be bent.

GOD

Abraham, my servant, Abraham!

ABRAHAM

Lo, Lord, already here I am.

GOD

Take Isaac, thy loved little lamb
In whom thy heart takes all delight
And cut his throat upon yon height
In sacrifice his blood to spill.
With sword and fire upon yon hill
Abraham, thy son Isaac must thou kill.

ABRAHAM

My Lord, to thee is mine intent
Ever to be obedient.
That son that thou to me hast sent
Offer I will to thee.
High God, lord omnipotent,
Thy bidding, Lord, done shall be.

(To ISAAC)

Make thee ready, my dear darling,
For we must do a little thing.
This wood do thou on thy back bring
We may no longer bide.
A sword and fire that I will take
For sacrifice me behoves to make.
God's bidding will I not forsake
But ever obedient be.

(ABRAHAM takes fire and sword.
ISAAC takes up the firewood, a spar of Noah's ark.)

ISAAC

Father I all ready
To do your bidding most meekely,
And to bear this wood full bowne am I
As ye commanded me.

ABRAHAM

O Isaac, my darling dear,
My blessing now I give thee here.
Take up this faggot with good cheer
And on thy back it bring.
And fire with us I will take.

ISAAC

Your bidding I will not forsake;
Father, haste now will I make
To fulfil your bidding.

ABRAHAM

Now Isaac, son, go we our way
To yonder mount, if that we may.
O my heart will break in three!
To hear thy words I have pity.
As thou wilt, Lord, so must it be.

(They proceed to the top of the hill. Enter BUTCHERS *with a butcher's block for altar.* BUTCHERS *sharpen knives rhythmically.)*

ISAAC

All ready, father, lo it here.
But why make ye so heavy cheer?
Are ye any thing adread?
Father, if it be thy will,
Where is the beast that we shall kill?

ABRAHAM

Thereof, son, is none upon the hill
That I see here upon this stead.

ISAAC

(Becoming afraid)

Father, I am full sore afraid
To see you bear that sharpened knife
I hope by all my tender life
You will not slay your child.

ABRAHAM

Dread thee not, my child, I read
Our Lord will send of his godhead
Some manner of beast into this field,
Either tame or wild.

ISAAC

Father, tell me or I go
Whether I shall harm or no.

ABRAHAM

Ah dear God, that me is woe!
Thou bursts my heart in sunder.

ISAAC

Father, tell me of this case:
Why you your sword outdrawn has,
And bears it naked in this place.
Thereof I have great wonder.

ABRAHAM

Isaac, son, peace, I pray thee.
Thou breakest my heart anon in three.

ISAAC

I pray you, father, hide nothing from me,
But tell me what you think.

ABRAHAM

Ah, Isaac, Isaac, I must thee kill.

ISAAC

Alas, father, is that your will
Your own child for to spill
Upon this hill's steep brink.

If I have trespassed in any degree
With a stick you may beat me.
Put up your sword if your will be
For I am but a child.

ABRAHAM

O my dear son, I am sorry
To do to thee this great annoy.
God's commandment do must I;
His works are ay full mild.

ISAAC

Is it God's will I shall be slain?

ABRAHAM

Son, I cannot hide from you
It is God's bidding I must do.

ISAAC

Then you must do what God has bid.
But tell not my mother what you did.

ABRAHAM

O Isaac, Isaac, blessed must thou be!
Almost my wit I lose for thee.
The blood of thy body so free
I am full loth to shed.

ISAAC

(Kneeling)

Father, since you must needs do so,
Let it pass lightly and over go.
Kneeling upon my knees too
Your blessing on me spread.

ABRAHAM

My blessing, dear son, give I thee,
And thy mother's with heart so free.
The blessing of the Trinity,
My dear son, on thee light.

ISAAC

Father, I pray you hide my eyen
That I see not the sword so keen.

Your stroke, father, would I not spy
Lest I against it scream and cry.

ABRAHAM

My dear son Isaac, speak no more;
The words make my heart full sore.

ISAAC

O dear father, wherefore, wherefore?
Since I must needs be dead,
Of one thing I would you pray.
Since I must die the death today,
As few strokes as ye well may
When ye smite off my head.

ABRAHAM

Thy meekness, child, makes me affray;
My song may be 'O well away'.

ISAAC

O dear father, do away, do away
Your making of much moan.
Now truly, father, this talking
Doth but make long tarrying.
I pray you come and make ending
And let me hence be gone.

ABRAHAM

Come hither, my child, thou art so sweet.
Thou must be bounden hand and feet.

(ABRAHAM *binds* ISAAC *and hoists him on to the altar.*)

ISAAC

Father, we must no moe meet
By ought that I can see.
God's commandment ye must fulfil
For needs so must it be.
But, father, I cry you mercy
For all that ever I have trespassed to thee;

46

Forgiven, father, that it may be
Until Doomsday.

ABRAHAM

My dear son, let be thy moans.
Blessed be thou, body and bones
And I forgive thee here.
Now, my dear son, here shall thou lie.
Unto my work now must I hie.
I had as lief myself to die
As thou, my darling dear.

ISAAC

Father, if ye be to me kind
About my head a kerchief bind
And let me lightly out of your mind
And soon that I were sped.

ABRAHAM

Farewell, my sweet son of grace!

ISAAC

I pray you, father, turn down my face
A little while, if you have space,
For I am full sore adread.

ABRAHAM

Heart, if thou would break in three,
Thou shalt never master me.
I will no longer let for thee.
My God I may not grieve.

ISAAC

A mercy, Father! Why tarry you so?
Smite off my head, and let me go!
I pray you rid me of my woe;
For now I take my leave.

ABRAHAM

Ah, son, my heart will break in three
To hear thee speak such words to me.
Jesu, on me thou have pity
That I have most in mind.

ISAAC

Now, father, I see that I shall die.
Almighty God in majesty
My soul I offer unto thee;
Lord, to it be kind.

(ABRAHAM *raises the sword and is about to strike off* ISAAC'S *head when* GOD *intervenes.*)

GOD

Abraham, hold back thy hand
And spare to spill thine Isaac's blood.
All that thy God did command
Thou didst, obedient and good.

Thy son is spared, but understand
That I mine own son, free of sin,
Will sacrifice to break that band
The Devil has all mankind within.
Thy son I spared thee for to spill.
Like thine Isaac, my loved lad
Shall do full heartily his Father's will,
But *not* be spared strokes sore and sad,
But done to death upon a hill.

(*The* BUTCHERS *perform a sword dance and the 'Star of David' is created. Song: 'Everything you do'. Exeunt.*)

BAND

Everything you do
You do for me
Everything you do you do for me.

(*Words and music: Richard Thompson*)

The Annunciation

ANGEL GABRIEL *appears above.*

ANGEL GABRIEL
Sirs, Isaie says a maiden young
Shall bear a son among Hebrews
That of all countries shall be king,
And govern all that on earth grows.
'Emmanuel' shall be his name –
To say, God's son in heaven.

(Angel music. Enter JOSEPH.*)*

JOSEPH
I am beguiled; how, know I not.
My young wife is with child full great;
That makes me now sorrow unsought.
The child certes is not mine;
That reproof does me pine
And gars me flee from home.
My life though I resign,
She is a clean virgin
For me, withouten blame.
But well I wit through prophecy
A maiden clean should bear a child . . .
But yet it is not so, surely,
Because I wit I am beguiled.
Nevertheless 'tis my intent
To ask her who got her her bairn –
That would I fain wit ere I went.
All hail! God be herein.

(Enter MARY.*)*

MARY
Welcome, as God me speed;
Doubtless to me he is full dear.
Joseph, my spouse, welcome are ye.

JOSEPH

Gramercy, Mary. Say, what cheer?
Tell me in sooth, how is't with thee?
Who has been there?
Thy womb is waxen great, think me.
Thou art with bairn, alas! For care.
Whose is't, Mary?

MARY

Sir, God's and yours.

JOSEPH

Whe! Why gab ye at me so?
And feign such fantasy?
Alas, me is full woe;
For dole might I not die?
To me this is a careful case;
Reckless I rave; rest is my rede.
I dare look no man in the face;
For heavy dole would I were dead;
Me loathe my life.
Whose is the child thou art withal?

MARY

Yours, sir, and the king's of bliss.

JOSEPH

Thou art young and I am old;
Such works if I do would,
These games from me are gone.
Therefore tell me in privity,
Whose is the child thou art with now?

MARY

(Appealing to ANGEL GABRIEL)

Now great God of his might,
That all may dress and dight,
Meekly to thee I bow.
Rue on this weary wight,

That in his heart may light
The truth to ken and know.

JOSEPH

Who had thy maidenhead, Mary? Has thy aught mind.

MARY

Forsooth, I am a maiden clean.

JOSEPH

Nay, thou speakest now against kind.
Such thing might no man signify –
A maiden to be with child!
These words from thee are wild –
She is not born, I ween.

MARY

Joseph, you are beguiled.
With sin was I never defiled.
God's sending is on me seen.

JOSEPH

God's sending? Yah, Mary! God help!

(Music. ANGEL *appears.)*

BAND

Shay fan yan lay
Shay fan yan lay
Shay fan yan lay
Yrie ralt nah maginah gow
In mannan hyum.

ANGEL GABRIEL

I Gabriel am; God's angel I,
That have taken Mary to my keeping,
And sent to thee aloud to cry,
In leal wedlock lead thee.
Leave her not, I forbid thee;
No sin of her imply,
But to her fast thou speed thee;

51

And of her nought thou dread thee.
God's word this, from on high:
The child that shall be born of her,
It is conceived of the Holy Ghost.
All joy and bliss then shall be after,
And to mankind of all the most.
Jesus his name thou call;
Such hap shall him befall,
As thou shalt see in haste.
His people save he shall
Of evils and angers all
That they are now embraced.

Wend forth to Mary thy wife all ways.
Bring her to Beth'lem this ilk night.
There shall a child born be;
God's son of heaven is he
And man aye most of might.

JOSEPH

Yea, Mary. I am to blame
For words long since I to thee spake.
But gather up now all our gear,
Such worn weeds as we wear.
And press them in a pack.
To Beth'lem must I it bear,
For little things will women fear.
Help up now, on my back.

(Music: Nativity.)

Now would I fain we had some light,
    What so befall.
It wakes right murk unto my sight,
    And cold withal.
I will go get us light this tide,
And fuel find with me to bring.

(Candles lit. Song: 'Lay Me Low'.)

BAND

Lay me low
Lay me low
Lay me low
Where no one can see me
Where no one can find me
Where no one can hurt me.

Show me the way
Help me to say
All that I need to
All that I needed you gave me
All that I wanted you made me
When I stumbled you saved me.

Lay me low
Lay me low
Lay me low
Where no one can see me
Where no one can find me
Where no one can hurt me.

(Words and Music: John Tams (adapted from a Shaker hymn). Published by Island Music.)

JOSEPH

Ah, Lord God! What light is this
That comes shining thus suddenly?

MARY

You are welcome, sir.

JOSEPH

Say, Mary daughter, what cheer with thee?

MARY

Right good, Joseph as has been aye.

JOSEPH

Oh, Mary – what sweet thing is that on thy knee?

MARY

It is my son, the sooth to say.
That is so good.

JOSEPH

Now welcome, flower fairest of hue,
I shall thee marvel main and might.
Hail, my Maker! Hail, Christ Jesu!
Hail, royal king, root of all right!
Hail Saviour!
Hail, my Lord, leamer of light!
Hail, blessed floor!

(Reprise of song. Candles blown out.
Enter HEROD, *fanfare.)*

BAND

Here is our King, his icy heart it holds us.
Here is our King, his iron fist enfolds us.
His sword is law, his aim is mighty.
Herod is our King
Herod is our King
Herod is our King   Herod!

(Words and music: Bill Caddick)

HEROD

The clouds clapped in clearness that their climates
encloses,
Jupiter and Jovis, Martis et Mercurii amid,
Raking over my royalty on row me rejoices,
Blustering their blasts, to blow when I bid.
Saturn my subject, that subtly is hid,
I list at my liking, and lay him full low.
The racke of the red sky full rapidly I rid:
Thunders full thraley by thousands I throw
When me likes.
Her voice to me Venus did owe,
That princes to play in her pikes.

The prince of the planets that proudly is pight
Shall brace forth his beams that our shelter shall know;
The moon at my might, he musters his might;
And kaisers in castles great kindness me show.
Lords and ladies as lovers list, lo,
For I am fairer of face and fresher, I hold,
(The sooth, if I shall say) seven and six fold,
My glorious gules that gayer is than God's gold
    In price.
How think ye, these tales that I told?
I am worthy, witty, and wise.

My son that is seemly and as such like his sire
He's learned in Latin and full lovely of lyre.
I'm bold, the blood-shedder, my bairn has the brains.

SON

All hail, pater most potent who right royally reigns
And beats down all rebels with blows from his brand.

HEROD

Hail, lad, my adviser, most learned in t'land
Come close to thy father and clasp thou my hand.

(They shake hands.)

SON

He's mighty in muscle . . .

HEROD

            He's mighty in mind

BOTH

Betwixt and between us we master mankind.

SON

He rules and wields power.

HEROD

            He can read, he can write
With his mind . . .

SON

> and his muscle . . .

BOTH

> we maintain our
> might.

HEROD

All those agen us get donged down and done
By t'buxom . . .

SON

and brainy . . .

HEROD

> Herod . . .

SON

> and son!

(Exeunt HEROD *and* SON.
Enter the THREE KINGS, *to observe their annual prayer and starwatch on the mountain.)*

KING 1

Well we wot, forsooth I wis,
That Balaam's prophecy sooth is –
A star should rise to token bliss
When God's son is born.
Therefore these lords and I all here
On this mount make we our prayer
Devoutly once in every year
For thereto have we sworn.

(The THREE KINGS *pray.)*

Lord, what time is it thy will
Balaam's prophecy to fulfil,
Give us some sign now on this hill.

KING 2

Lord God, leader of Israel
That die would for mankind's heal,
Thou come to us and not conceal.

KING 3

Yea, Lord, show they mercy
On my realm, rich Araby
And of thy birth now certify
Here and now to thy kings three.

(*The* THREE KINGS *consult the heavens, and finally find the star.*)

KING 1

Ah, Lord, blessed must thou be,
That on thy people has pity
And lets us now yon star to see.

KING 2

That our prayer heard has he
I believe full well, by my lewtee,
For in the star a child I see.

KING 3

Lords, I read we heathen hie
For I dare say and nothing lie
Fulfilled is Balaam's prophecy.

KING 1

Lords, hie we heathen then anon
Now we been bidden thither gone.
I will never bide, by my bonne,
Till I at him be.

KING 2

Yea, sirs, I read us everyone
Dromedaries to ride upon,
For swifter beasts there be none.
One I have, ye shall see.

KING 3

A dromedary, in good fay,
Will go lightly on his way
An hundred miles upon a day.
Such beasts now take we.

(The THREE KINGS *journey on their dromedaries following the star. Then they lose it.*)

KING 1

Alas, where is this star iwent.
Our light from us away is glent.
Witherward lies our way?

KING 2

God to whom we bring present
Will never suffer us to be shent,
That dare I boldly say.

KING 3

It is good that we enquire
If any the way can us lere.

(*Enter* MESSENGER.)

Say, bel ami, that rides there
Tell us some tiding.

MESSENGER

Sirs, tell me what your will were.

KING 1

Can thou ought say what place or where
A child is born that crown shall bear
And of the Jews be king?

KING 2

We saw the star shine, veray!
In the east in noble array.
Therefore we come now this way
To find the palace he dwells in.

MESSENGER

Hold your peace, sirs, I you pray.
For if King Herod hear you so say
He might go mad, by my fay,
And fly out of his skin.

KING 2

Then since a great king dwells in this street
Let us three lords now go him greet.

(*Exeunt* KINGS *to Wise Men's music.*
Enter 1ST, 2ND *and* 3RD SHEPHERDS.)

1ST SHEPHERD

But we silly farm-hands   that walk on the moor,
In faith we are near-hands   turned out of door.

2ND SHEPHERD

No wonder, as it stands   if we be poor,
For the tilth of our lands   lies fallow as a floor,
    As ye ken.

1ST SHEPHERD

We are so ham-bound.

2ND SHEPHERD

Over-taxed.

1ST SHEPHERD

        And down-ground;
We have no rights allowed
        By these gentry-men.

3RD SHEPHERD

Ah, sir, God you save,   and you master mine!
A drink fain would I have,   and on somewhat to dine.

1ST SHEPHERD

Christ's curse, my lazy knave,   your belly will regret it!

2ND SHEPHERD

How the boy loves to rave!   And any road we've ate it.

1ST SHEPHERD

Aye. By the rood,   these nights are long!
Yet. I wish, ere we go,   someone gave us a song.

(Song: 'Shepherd's Round'.)

BAND

Whose tups are these?
Whose tups are these?
They're old Jack Bourne's
I can tell 'em by their horns
And I found 'em in the vicarage garden.

(Traditional, adapted by John Tams. Published by Island Music.)

(Enter MAK *with a fine cloak worn over his tunic.)*

1ST SHEPHERD

Who is't that peeps so poor?

MAK

Lo, a man that walks on the moor,
    And all unwillingly.

2ND SHEPHERD

Mak, where has thou gone?   Tell us tidings.

3RD SHEPHERD

Is *he* come? Then each one   take heed of his things.

(He shakes MAK'S *cloak.)*

MAK

What! I be a yeoman,   I tell you, of the king's,
The selfsame one,   messenger of great laudings.
I shall make complaint;   and get you many a thwang
    Without another word.

1ST SHEPHERD

Mak, now take out that Southern tooth
    And put in a turd.

MAK

Nay, lads; it's only me thou knows,
How goes you; how's the herd?

2ND SHEPHERD

    Look out villain!
Thus late as thou goes
What will men suppose?
We've heard ill news
    Of sheep stealing.

MAK

And I am true as steel,   as all men do wit;
But a sickness I feel,   that holds me full hot;
My belly fares not well: it is quite out of its state.

3RD SHEPHERD

Seldom lies the devil   dead by the gate.

MAK

Therefore, full sore am I and ill;
If I stand stone still.
I ate not an needle
    This month and more.

2ND SHEPHERD

Mak, how fares thy wife?   By thy hood, how does she
                              do?

MAK

Lies lathering by the fire,   waltering, lo!
And the house full of our brood.   She drinks well, too;
Ill-speed all other good   that she wish to do!
    And so
Eats as fast as she can
And each year that comes to man

She brings forth an infant,
　　And some years two.

But were I now more gracious　and richer by far,
I were eaten out of house　and out of harbour.
Yet is she a foul dowse,　if ye come near;
There is no man trows　worse, or knows more
　　Than ken I.
Now will ye see what I proffer? –
To give all in my coffer
At tomorrow's mass to offer
　　A penny, should she die.

2ND SHEPHERD

I wot so weary with waking　is none in this shire;
I would sleep,　were I taking less to my hire.

3RD SHEPHERD

I am cold and am shaking,　and would have a fire.

1ST SHEPHERD

I am worn out with walking,　and deep in the mire –
　　Keep awake you!

(He lies down.)

2ND SHEPHERD

　　Nay, I will lie down by,
　　For I must sleep, truly.

(Lies down too.)

3RD SHEPHERD

　　As good a man's son was I
　　　As any of you.

But Mak, come hither!　between us shall thou lie.

(He does the same and makes MAK *do so.)*

MAK

　　Then might I hinder　the quiet words you may try;
　　So take heed.

From my top to my toe,
Manus tuas commendo,
Pontio Pilato!
    Christ's cross me speed.

(The SHEPHERDS *sleep; and then* MAK *rises. The* SHEPHERDS *snore.)*

Lord, how they sleep hard!   That may ye all hear.
I was never a shepherd,   but now will I learn.
If the flock be scared,   yet shall I nip near.
Ho! Draw hitherward!   Now mends all our cheer
    From sorrow,
A fat sheep, I dare say,
A good fleece, dare I lay.
Pay back when I may,
    But this will I borrow.

(He goes home with the sheep. The SHEPHERDS *awake.)*

1ST SHEPHERD
Alas, that ever I was born!   We have a foul blot.
A fat wedder have we lorn.

3RD SHEPHERD
            Marry, God forbot!
Now trust me, if ye will;   by Saint Thomas of Kent
Either Mak or Gill,   to that gave assent.

Go we hither, as I rede,   and run on our feet.
Shall I never eat bread,   the sooth till I weet.

(Exits.)

1ST SHEPHERD
Nor drink in my head,   with him till I meet.

(Exits.)

2ND SHEPHERD
I will rest in no stead,   till that I him greet.

(Exits.)

(Enter MAK *at his house.)*

MAK

Ho! Gill, art thou in?   Get us some light.

WIFE

Who makes such a din   this time of the night?

MAK

Good wife, open up quick! Sees thou not what I
bring?

WIFE

I will let thee draw the sneck.   Ah, come in my
sweeting!

*(*MAK *shows her the sheep.)*

MAK

Thus it fell to my lot, Gill;   I had such grace.

WIFE

It were a foul blot   to be hanged for that case.

MAK

I wish it were slain;   I list well to eat:
This twelvemonth was I not so fain   for a slice of
sheep-meat.

WIFE

Come they ere it be slain,   and hear the sheep
bleat . . .

MAK

Then might I be tane.   That were a cold sweat!
    Go barr
The back door.

WIFE

A good jest have I spied,   since thou can find none:
Here shall we him hide,   until they be gone,
In my cradle.   Abide!   Let me alone,

And I shall sit down beside   as in childbed, and
groan.

This is a good guise,   and a far-cast;
Still a woman's advice   helps at the last.

MAK

The last word that they said   when I turned my back:
They would look that they had   their sheep, all the
pack.
I think they will not be well pleased   when they their
sheep lack.

WIFE

Harken for when they call;   they will come at once.
Come, and make ready all,   and sing on thine own;
Sing 'Lullaby' thou shall,   for I must groan,
And cry out by the wall,   on Mary and John.
Full sore.

(The sheep bleats. Enter SHEPHERDS *and knock on the door.)*

MAK

Why, sir, ails ye aught but good?

1ST SHEPHERD

Yea, our sheep that
we get
Are stolen as they go.   Our loss is great.

2ND SHEPHERD

Mak, some men suppose   that it should be thee.

3RD SHEPHERD

Either thee or thy spouse,   so say we.

MAK

Now if ye have suppose   to Gill or to me,
Come rip open our house,   and then may ye see
Who had her.
If I any sheep got

65

Either female or stod –
And Gill, my wife, rose not
    Here since she laid her –

As I am true and loyal,   to God here I pray
That this be the first meal   that I shall eat this day.

(He points to the cradle. The sheep bleats.)

WIFE

    Ooh!   My middle!
I pray to God so mild,
If ever I ye beguild,
That I *eat* this child
    That lies in this cradle.

MAK

Peace, woman, for God's pain,   and cry not so!
Thou spills all thy brain,   and makes me full woe.

2ND SHEPHERD

I trow our sheep be slain.   What find ye two?

3RD SHEPHERD

All work we in vain: as well may we go.
    Only tatters!
I can find no flesh,
Hard or nesh,
Salt or fresh –
    Only two empty platters.

(Pointing to cradle)

Living beast besides this,   tame or wild,
None, as have I bliss,   strong though it smelled.

WIFE

No. So God gi' me bliss.   And give me joy of my child!

1ST SHEPHERD

We have marked amiss.   I hold us beguild.

2ND SHEPHERD

Sir, we've done.
But Sir – our Lady him save! –
Is your child girl or knave?

MAK

Ay lord might him have,
    This child, to his son.

2ND SHEPHERD

Mak, friends will we be,   for we are all one.

MAK

We? Now I hold back, me,   for amends get I none.
Fare well all three!   *(aside)* All glad were ye gone.

(The SHEPHERDS *leave the house.)*

3RD SHEPHERD

Fair words may there be,   but love is there none
    This year.

1ST SHEPHERD

Gave ye the child anything?

2ND SHEPHERD

I trow not one farthing.

3RD SHEPHERD

Fast again will I fling:
    Abide ye me there.

(The SHEPHERDS *return.)*

Mak, take it to no grief   if I come to thy bairn.

MAK

Nay, thou does me great reproof,   and foul thyself
                                    borne.

3RD SHEPHERD

The child will not grieve,   that little day-starne.

67

Mak, with your leave,   let me give your bairn
    But six pence.

MAK

Nay, have done.   He sleeps.

3RD SHEPHERD

Methinks he peeps.

MAK

When he wakens he weeps.
    I pray you go hence!

3RD SHEPHERD

Give me leave him to kiss,   and lift up the clout.
What the devil is this?   He has a long snout!

1ST SHEPHERD

He is marked amiss.   We should not pry about.

2ND SHEPHERD

Ill-spun weft, I wis,   ever comes foul out.
    Aye, so!
He is like to our sheep.

3RD SHEPHERD

Ho, Gib, may I peep?

1ST SHEPHERD

I trow nature will creep
    Where it may not go.

2ND SHEPHERD

This was a quaint gaud,   and a far-cast;
It was a fine fraud.

3RD SHEPHERD
                Yea, sirs, was't.
Let us burn this bawd   and bind her fast.
A false scald   does hand at the last;
    So shall thou.
Will ye see how they swaddle

His four feet in the middle?
Saw I never in a cradle
    A horned lad ere now.

MAK

Peace, bid I. What,   let be your uproar!
I am he that him gat,   and yond woman him bare.

2ND SHEPHERD

Let be all that!   Now God send him care!
    I saw.

WIFE

As pretty child is he,
As e'er sits on woman's knee;
A dillydon, perdy,
    To cause a man laugh.

3RD SHEPHERD

I know him by the ear-mark: that is a sure token.

MAK

I tell you, sirs – hark! –   his nose was broken.
And then told me a clerk   that witchcraft had spoken.

1ST SHEPHERD

This was a false work;   revenge must be wreaken.
    Get weapon!

WIFE

He was taken by an elf;
I saw it myself.
When the clock struck twelve
    Was he forshapen.

2ND SHEPHERD

Ye two are both deft,   and belong in one stead.

1ST SHEPHERD

Since they maintain their theft,   let us do them to
                          death.

MAK

If I trespass here aft',   strike off my head.
With you the matter be left.

3RD SHEPHERD
                              Sirs, do my rede:
    For this trespass
We will neither ban nor flite,
Fight nor chide
But have done forthright.
Set yon sheep thief in t'stocks
        And small folk on this floor
Take sopping wet sponges and splash him full sore.

(Children in the audience are encouraged to throw wet sponges at
MAK *in the stocks.)*

1ST SHEPHERD
Lord, how I am sore,   at point for to burst!
In faith, I can no more;   therefore will I rest.

2ND SHEPHERD
As a sheep of seven score   he weighed in my fist.
For to sleep anywhere   methink that I list.

3RD SHEPHERD
    Now I pray you
Lie down on this ground.

1ST SHEPHERD
These thieves stay still in my mind.

3RD SHEPHERD
Wherefore should ye be pained?
    Do as I say you.

BAND
Shay fan yan lay
Shay fan yan lay
Shay fan yan lay

Yrie ralt nah maginah grow
In mannan hyum.

(They lie down to sleep. The ANGEL *enters above.)*

ANGEL

Hark, herdsmen! Awake!   Give worship ye shall:
He is born for your sake,   lord perpetual.
He is comen to take   and ransom you all;
Your sorrow to slake,   king imperial,
  He behests.
That child is born
At Bethlehem this morn:
Ye shall find him beforn,
  Betwixt two beasts.

1ST SHEPHERD

Ah, God's dear *Dominus*!   What was that song?
I was wonder curious,   with small notes among.
I pray to God, save us   now in this throng!
I am 'feard, by Jesus,   somewhat be wrong.
  Methought
One screamed aloud:
I suppose it was a cloud;
In my ears it soughed,
  By him that me bought!

2ND SHEPHERD

Nay, that may not be,   I say you certain,
For he spake to us three   as he had been a man.
When he lightened this lea;   my heart shaked then:
An angel was he – tell you I can –
  No doubt.
He spake of a bairn.
We must seek him, I warn:
That betokens yond starne
  That stands yonder out.

(He points to the sky.)

3RD SHEPHERD

It was marvel to see,   so bright as it shone
I   would   have   trowed,   verily,   it   had   been
thunderflown,
But I saw with mine eye   as I leaned to this stone.
It was a merry glee,   such heard I never none,
I record,
As he said in a scream –
Or els that I dream –
We should go to Bed'leme,
To worship that lord.

(Exeunt.
Enter HEROD, SON *and* MESSENGER.*)*

MESSENGER

My lord sir Herod, king with crown –

HEROD

Peasse, dastard, in the devil's despite.

MESSENGER

Sir, new affair is near this town.

HEROD

What, false losel? List thee flight?
Go beat yon boy and ding him down.

SON

Father, I shall fell him in fight
That rogue that would reave you of your right.

MESSENGER

Lord, messengers should no man smite;
It may be for your own renown.

HEROD

That would I hear. Do tell on, tight.

MESSENGER

My lord, I met at morn

Three kings carping together
Of one that is now born;
And they hight to come hither.

HEROD

Three kings, forsooth?

MESSENGER

          Sir, so I say,
For I saw them myself all clear.

SON

My Father, examine him, we pray.

HEROD

Say, fellow, are they far or near?

MESENGER

My lord, they will be here this day;
That wot I well. No doubt is here.

HEROD

Have done! Dress us in rich array,
And every man make merry cheer,
That no semblance be seen
But friendship fair and still,
Till we wot what they mean,
Whether it be good or ill.

(Puts on costume.)

(Enter THREE KINGS *to Herod's court.* SON *acts as 'interpreter'.)*

KING 1

Syr roy, ryall and reverent
Deu vous gard, omnipotent.

KING 2

Nos sommes veneus comoplent
Novelis de enquire

HEROD

(Prompted by his SON*)*

> Bien soies venues, royes gents,
> Me detes tout votere entent.

KING 3

Infant querenues de grand parent
Et roi de celi et de terre.

HEROD

Sirs, avise you what you say
Such tidings break my heart they may.

I am the king of all mankind.
I bide, I beat, I loose, I bind.
I master the moon. Take this in mind –
That I am most of might.

KING 1

Sir, by prophecy well witten we
That a child born should be
To rule the people of Judee.

HEROD

Since ye speak of prophecy,
My son here soon shall see
Whether ye speak sooth or lie,
My son, the Doctor of Philosophy.

(To SON*)*

> Look up thy books of prophecy
> Of Daniel, David, and Isaye
> And what thou seeest say thou me.
> Seek each leaf I thee pray
> And tell me here, for I dare lay
> That all these lords lie, they lie.

*(*SON *consults York telephone directory and reads rapidly in Latin.)*

SON

'Non auferetur sceptrum de Juda et dux de foemere
eius, donec veniet qui mittendus est et erit ipse
expectation gentium.'

(SON *shakes his head. The* KINGS *don't lie.*)

HEROD

(*Grabs* SON *in anger*)
   False, all false, by Mahowne of might.
   Any shitty-arse shrew that robs me of right
   His head off shall I hew. Yet seek in thy book
   Whether that boy is born for whom these lords look.

SON

(*Reading rapidly*)
   'Et tu Bethlem quidem terra Juda nequaquam minima
   et in principibus Judae. Ex te enim exiet dux qui reget
   populum meum Israell.'

(SON *nods assent much to the fury of* HEROD.)

HEROD

   I shall hew that harlot with my bright brand so keen
   Into pieces small. Yet look and search again
   If these kings shall him find and his presence attain.

SON

(*Reading rapidly*)
   'Reges Tharsis et Insule munera offerent; reges
   Arabum et Saba dona adducent. Psalmo septuagesimo
   primo.'

(SON *nods assent. Yes, they will find him.*
HEROD *rips the book into pieces.*)

HEROD

   By cock's soul! Thou art forsworn.
   Have done. Now thy books are rent and torn.

   This realm is mine and shall be ay
   Manfully master it while I may.

But go you forth, you kings three
And enquire if it so be.
But algates come again by me
For you I think to feed.
And if he be of such degree,
Hin will I honour as do ye,
As falls for his dignity
In word, thought and deed.

KING 1

By your leave, sir, and have good day
Til we come again this way.

HEROD

Farewell, lords, in good fay,
But hie you fast again this way.

(Bows.
Exeunt THREE KINGS.*)*

My Mahound, come they again
All three traitors shall be slain,
And that same swaddling swain
I shall chop off his head.

This boy doth me so greatly annoy
That I wax dull and pure dry.
Have done and fill the wine in high
I die but I have a drink!
Fill fast and let the cups fly
And go we heathen hastily
For I must ordain curiously
Against these kings' coming.

(Exeunt HEROD *and* SON.*)*

The Stable

The SHEPHERDS *enter the stable singing the 'Coventry Carol'.*

SHEPHERDS
Lully lullay thou little tiny child
Bye, bye lully lullay
Lully lullay thou little tiny child
Bye, bye lully lullay.

(All kneel.)

1ST SHEPHERD
Hail, comely and clean!   Hail, young child!
Hail, maker, as I mean, of maiden so mild!
Thou has confounded, I ween,   the Warlock so wild:
The false bringer of teen,   now goes he beguiled.
    Lo, merry he is!
Lo, he laughs, my sweeting!
Ah! A very fair meeting!
I have held to my telling:
    Have a bob of cherries.

2ND SHEPHERD
Hail, sovereign saviour,   for thou hast us sought!
Hail, nurseling and flower, that all thing has
                              wrought!
Hail, full of favour,   that make all out of nought!
Hail! I kneel and I cower.   A bird have I brought
    To my bairn.
Hail, little tiny mop!
Of our creed thou art crop:
I would drink of thy cup,
    Little day-starne.

3RD SHEPHERD
Hail, little darling dear,   full of Godhead!
I pray thee be near   when that I have need.
Hail, sweet in thy cheer!   My heart will bleed

To see thee sit here   in so poor a weed,
    With no pennies.
Hail! Put forth thy dall.
I bring thee but a ball:
Have and play thee withall,
    And go to the tennis.

MARY

The father of heaven,   God omnipotent,
That set all in days seven,   his son has he sent.
My name could he namen,   and on me his light spent!
I conceived him full even   by God's might as he
                              meant;
    And now is he born.
May he keep you from woe!
I shall pray him so.
Tell forth as ye go,
    And mind on this morn.

(All stand.)

1ST SHEPHERD

Farewell lady,   So fair to behold,
With thy child on thy knee.

2ND SHEPHERD

    But he lies full cold.
Lord, it is well for me!   Now we go, thou behold.

(The THREE KINGS *enter.)*

KING 1

I hope without dread today
To see that child and his array.
But, methinks, lords, by my fay,
The star it standeth still.

KING 2

That is a sign that we be near.
But high hall see I none here.

To a child of such power
This housing standeth low.

1ST SHEPHERD

Whom seek ye, sirs, by ways so wild,
With talking, travelling to and fro?
Here dwells a woman with her child
And her husband; here are no mo.

KING 1

We seek a bairn that all shall shield;
His certain sign has said us so;
And his mother, a maiden mild.
Here hope we now to find them two.

1ST SHEPHERD

Come near, good sirs, and see.
Your way to an end is brought.

KING 3

What present best will for him fall
Cast we here among us all;
For though he lie in an ox stall
His might is none the less.

KING 1

Me beseemeth by this place
That little treasure his mother has.
Therefore to help her in this case
Gold present shall I.

KING 2

And I will offer through God's grace
Incense that noble savour has.
Stink of the stable it shall make pass
Where they both lie.

KING 3

And myrrh is best my offering to be
To anoint him, as thinks me,

The baby's members, head and knee,
Yea, all his bright body.

(He kneels and bows to baby.
Exeunt THREE KINGS.
MARY *and* JOSEPH *begin their journey.*
HEROD, SON *and* KNIGHT *enter.)*

HEROD

Oooh, by sun and moon,
Tidings will be told tonight.
Hope I those kings come soon
Hither, as they have hight,
Tidings me for to tell
Of where that shitty shrew
His dam just dropped doth dwell,
And his head off shall I hew.

SON

Nay, Father, that dance is done.

HEROD

Why, whither are they gone?

SON

Ilke one to their own land.

HEROD

How sayest thou, lad? Let be!

SON

I say, for they are past.

HEROD

What, forth away from me?

SON

Yea, lord, in faith full fast.
For I heard and took heed
How that they went all three
Into their own country.

HEROD

Ah, dogs! The devil them speed!

MESSENGER

Sir, more of their meaning
Yet well I understood;
How they made offering
Unto that child so good
That now of new is born;
They say he should be king.

HEROD

Alas, then am I lorn.
Fie on them, fakers, fie!
Will they beguile me thus?

MESSENGER

Lord, by their prophecy
They named his name Jesus.

HEROD

Thou liest, false traitor strong!
Look never thou nigh me near.
Upon life and limb,
May I that faker slay;
Full high I shall him hang,
Both thee, harlot, and him.

Alas, for sorrow and sight
My woe no wight may write.
What a devil is best to do?

SON

My lord, amend your cheer;
And take no needless 'noy.

HEROD

That may ye not come near.

MESSENGER

My Lord, now gather in great rout
Your knights so sharp to strive
To search in every stead
And seek that Jesus out
And ding him dead.

SON

Certes, that is well said
And seemeth sweet to me!

MESSENGER

What say you, lord? let see.

HEROD

To Beth'lem must ye wend,
That shrew with shame to shend
That means to master me.
Bide there till he be caught
And let me tell you how
Go work when ye come there;
Because you ken him not
To death must they be brought –
Knave children less and more
Yeah all within two year
That none for speech be spared.

(Exeunt.)

(JOSEPH with MARY on a 'donkey' holding the baby JESUS meet a group of MOTHERS with babies.)

SOLDIER 4
(Offstage)
Come forth, fellows; appear!

(Drum beat. Line of KNIGHTS and SATAN enter, three steps forward.)

SOLDIER 1
Lo, foundling, find we here.

(Drum beat. Line surrounds WOMEN. *They murder their babies.)*

1ST WOMAN

Out on you, thieves, I cry!
Ye slay my seemly son.

2ND WOMAN

Alas, this loathly strife!
No bliss may be my bete!
Alas, the knight upon his knife
Has slain my son so sweet!

1ST WOMAN

Alas lament I woe!
I wot the day is nigh:
The sayings that I know
Of Prophet Jeremy;
In Rama hear my cry.
Rachel's voice am I.
In wind and woe a-weeping:
No comfort will I buy
Since every child is sleeping.

KNIGHT

(To HEROD *and* SON)

Lord, they are dead,
Ilke one;
What would you we do more?

(HEROD *and* SON *laugh.* BAND *reprises 'Pride'.*
SOLDIERS *seat themselves at a table echoing 'The Last Supper')*

HERALD

My lord, the table is ready dight.
Here is water, now wash forthright.
Now blow up, minstrel, with all your might
The service cometh in soon.

HEROD

Now am I set at meat
And worthily served in my degree.
Come forth, knights, sit down to eat
And be as merry as ye can be.

SOLDIER 4

Lord at your bidding we take our seat
With hearty will obey we thee.
There is no lord of might so great
Through all this world in no country
In worship to abide.

HEROD

I was never merrier here beforn
Since that I was first born
Then I am now right in this morn.
In joy I gin to glide.

DEATH

Ow! I heard a page make pressing of pride!
All princes he passeth he weans of posté.
He weans to be worthiest of all this world wide.
King over all kings, that page weaneth to be.
He sent into Bethlem to seek on every side
Christ for to quell if they might him see.
But of his wicked will the lurdan he lied.
God's son doth live there is no lord but he.
Over all lords he is king.
I am death God's messenger.
Almighty God hath sent me here to
Yon lurdan to slay without more ado.

HEROD

Spare neither wine nor bread
For now I am king alone.
So worthy as I, may there be none.
Therefore, knights, be merry each one
For now my foe is dead.

SOLDIER 4

When the boys sprawled at my spear end
By Satan our sire it was a goodly sight.
A good game it was that boy for to shend
That would be our king and put you from your right.

SOLDIER 1

Yea, was it lovely to see those lads leap
On to our spear-tips and straightway to sleep.
All bawling babes in Bethlem at t'breast
Their naps know no ending, and thy realm knows rest.

HEROD

Amongst all that great rout
He is dead I have no doubt.
Therefore minstrels round about
Blow up a merry fit.

DEATH

I am sent from God – Death is my name
All thing that is on ground I wield at my will
Both man and beast and birds wild and tame
When I come them to, with death I do them kill.
Herb, grass and trees strong with my dents I spill.
What man that I wrestle with he shall right soon have
shame.
I give him such a trip up he shall ever more lie still.
For death can not sport
Where I smite there is no grace
For after my stroke man hath no space
To make amends for his trespass
But God him grant comfort.
Ow! See how proudly yon caitiff at meat he now sits
Of Death he hath no doubt. He weaneth to live for ever
more.
To him will I go and give him such hits
That all the leeches of the land his life shall ne'er
restore.

Against my dreadful dents no plea availeth yet.
Afore I him part fro I shall make him full pour
All the blood of his body I shall him out sweat.
For now I go to slay him with strokes sad and sore
Both him and his knights all
I shall them make to me thrall
With my spear slay them I shall
And so cast down his pride.

(*The* BAND *plays and* DEATH *kills* HEROD *and the* SOLDIERS.)

Each one in suchlike array, with death they shall be
dight.
And closed cold in clay, whether they be king or
knight.
For all their garments gay, that seemly were in sight
Their flesh shall fret away, with many a woeful wight.
Thus woefully such wormy wights
Shall gnaw these gay knights
Their lungs and their lights.
    Their heart shall fret in sunder
These masters most in mights
    Thus shall they be brought under

Your ruddiness so red, your lyre lilly like
Then shall be wan as lead, and stink as dog in dyke.

This space about us all, no corpse shall need as much.
The roof of thy hall, thy naked nose shall touch.

(DEATH *leads off* HEROD *and the* SOLDIERS *in a 'Dance of Death'.*)

COMPANY

Shepherds arise be not afraid,
With hasty steps prepare.
To David's city, sing on earth.
With our blessed infant there.
With our blessed infant there.
With our blessed infant there.

Sing sing all earth.
Sing sing all earth
Eternal praises sing.
To our redeemer,
To our redeemer,
And our heavenly king.

Laid in a manger, viewed a child.
Humility divine,
Sweet innocence sounds meek and mild.
Grace in his features shine.
Grace in his features shine.
Grace in his features shine.

For us a saviour came on earth.
For us his life he gave.
To save us from eternal death.
To raise us from the grave.
To raise us from the grave.
To raise us from the grave.

(*Enter* MARY *and* JOSEPH *with the child surrounded by the* COMPANY *with lanterns.*)

THE PASSION

CHARACTERS

JOHN BAPTIST
ANGEL
JESUS
BLIND MAN
POOR MAN
PHILIP
PETER
BURGHERS
JUDAS
MARCELLUS
ANDREW
JOHN
PILATE
PERCULA
CAYPHAS
ANNAS
FOUR KNIGHTS
MALCUS
WOMAN
BARABBAS
MARY MOTHER
MARY MAGDALENE
MARY SALOME
SIMON OF CYRENE
CENTURION

The COMPANY *in the various uniforms and overalls of carpenter,
painter, butcher, fireman, bus conductor, ticket collector,
fishmonger, miner, mechanic, meat-porter, cleaner, gas fitter,
construction worker, etc., help the audience as they arrive to their
places and talk to them. The* BAND *on the stage begin to play a
polka tune and some of the* COMPANY *dance to it, while others clap
in rhythm. After the polka the* BAND *sings 'All in the Morning'.*

BAND

It was on Christmas Day and all in the morning
Our Saviour was born and our Heavenly King.
And was not this a joyful thing?
And sweet Jesus we'll call him by name.

It was on the same day and all in the morning
The shepherds were led to our Heavenly King.
And was not this a joyful thing?
And sweet Jesus they called him by name.

It was on a Holy Day and all in the morning
They baptized our Saviour our Heavenly King.
And was this not a joyful thing?
And sweet Jesus they called him by name.

(Traditional: additional lyrics: John Tams.)

During the song three women from the COMPANY *and* JESUS
move into the pit among the audience, and the women help JESUS *to
don a simple, rough, oat-coloured robe over his overalls.* JOHN
BAPTIST, *also in a simple robe over working clothes, gets into
position on steps above the audience in the pit. The* COMPANY
moves into position for:

The Baptism of Jesus

(The COMPANY *unfolds a blue silk cloth to represent the water of
the River Jordan.)*

JOHN BAPTIST
Almighty God, and Lord, I say
Full wonderful is man's failing.

For if I preach them day by day,
And tell them, Lord, of thy coming
    That all has wrought,
Men are so dull that my preaching
    Serves for nought.

(*Addressing* JESUS *at the other side of the 'river'*)
When I have, Lord, in the name of thee
Baptised the folk in water clear,
Then have I said that after me
Shall he come that has more power
    Than I can boast
He shall give bapti'm more entire
    In fire and Ghost

(*The* COMPANY *kneels, holding the edges of the blue cloth and shakes it gently to create the flowing of the River Jordan.*)

Thus am I come in message right
And am forerunner in certain,
In witness-bearing of that light,
The which shall lighten every man
    That comes at hand
Into this world; now whoso can
    May understand.

(*An* ANGEL *appears at an upper level.*)

ANGEL
Now, John, tak tent what I shall say.
I bring thee tidings wonder good.
My Jesu shall come this day
From Galilee unto this flood
    Ye Jordan call.
Bapti'm to take mildly with mood,
    This day he shall.

(*The* ANGEL *disappears.*)

JOHN BAPTIST
But well I wot, bapti'm is ta'en

To wash and cleanse a man of sin;
And well I wot that sin is none
In him, without him or within.
    What needs he then
To be baptised for any sin,
    Like sinful men?

JESUS

John, kind of man is frail,
To which I have me knit,
But I shall show thee reasons two,
That thou shalt know by kindly wit
The cause why I have ordained so;
    And one is this –
Mankind may not unbaptised go
    To endless bliss.
And since myself have taken mankind,
Men shall me for their mirror make.
I have their doing in my mind,
And so I do this bapti'm take.
    I will thereby
Myself be baptised for this sake
    Full openly.

JOHN BAPTIST

Lord, methinks it were more need
    Thou baptised me.

JESUS

Thou sayest full well, John certainly.
But suffer now, that righteousness
Be fulfilled not in word only
    But als' in deed,
    Through bapti'm clear.
Come, baptise me in my manhood
    Now and here.

(JOHN BAPTIST *rises.* JESUS *moves towards him.*)

JOHN BAPTIST

Ah, Lord; I tremble where I stand,
I am afeard to do that deed.
But save me, Lord that all ordained,
For thee to touch have I great dread,
    For doings dark.
Now help me, Lord, through thy godhead,
    To do this work.
Jesu, my Lord of mights the most,
I baptise thee here in the name
Of the Father and of the Son and Holy Ghost.

(The blue cloth is waved over the head of JESUS, *who is thus immersed in the River Jordan.* JESUS *rises. Three men raise* JOHN BAPTIST *high into the air.)*

Now, sirs, that bairn that Mary bore
    Be with you all.

(Music. Exit the COMPANY.*)*

The Entry into Jerusalem

Music. The BAND *leads a procession of the* COMPANY *who leave by one exit into the foyer, where they put on the robes of disciples. Only the actors who are to play the* BLIND MAN *and the* POOR MAN *remain.*

BLIND MAN

Ah lord, that all this world has made,
Both sun and moon and night and day,
What noise is this that makes me glad?
From whence it comes I cannot say,
    Or what it mean.
If any man walk in this way,
    Say what is seen.

POOR MAN

Why, man, what ails thee so to cry?
Where would thou be? Now tell me here.

BLIND MAN

Ah, sir, a poor blind man am I,
And aye have been from tender year,
    Since I was born.
I heard a voice of noble cheer,
    Here me before.

POOR MAN

Man, wilt thou ought that I can do?

BLIND MAN

Yea, sir; for gladly would I wit,
If thou would ought declare me true
This mirth I heard, what mean may it?
    Dost understand?

POOR MAN

Jesu the prophet full of grace
    Comes here at hand,
And all the citizens from town
Go him to meet with melody,
With the fairest procession
That was ever seen in this Jewry.
    He is right near.

BLIND MAN

Sir, help me to the street hastily,
    That I may hear
That noise, and that I might through grace –
My sight of him to crave I would.

(THREE WOMEN *enter and unroll a long rubber darts mat to serve as the path of strewn palms. The* THIRD WOMAN *sweeps the mat once it is unrolled.*
The POOR MAN *goes to the* BLIND MAN *to lead him into the pit to meet* JESUS. *The* COMPANY *enters with four men carrying* JESUS *seated on a wooden donkey. The* BAND *leads the procession.)*

POOR MAN

Lo, he is here at this same place.
Cry fast on him; look thou be bold,
　　With voice right high.

BLIND MAN

Jesu, Thou Son of David called,
　　Have thou mercy.
Alas! I cry, he hears me not;
He has no ruth for my misfare.
He turns his ear. Where is his thought?

POOR MAN

Cry somewhat louder; do not spare.
　　So may you speed.

BLIND MAN

Jesu, thou salver of all sore,
　　To me give good heed.

PHILIP

Cease, man, and cry not so.
The prince of the people goes thee by.
Thou should sit still and attend thereto.
Here passes the prophet of mercy;
　　Thou dost amiss.

BLIND MAN

Ah, David's son, to thee I cry,
　　The king of bliss.

PETER

Lord, have mercy and let him go;
He cannot cease of his crying;
He follows us both to and fro;
Grant him his boon and his asking
　　And let him wend.
We get no rest until this thing
　　Be brought to end.

JESUS

What wouldst thou, man, I to thee did?
In this presence, tell openly.

BLIND MAN

(*Kneeling*)
Lord, mine eyesight from me is hid;
Grant it to me, I cry mercy.
This would I have.

JESUS

Look up now with cheer blithely.
Thy faith can save.

(*The* BLIND MAN *looks up slowly and takes in the newly opened world of sight. The* BLIND MAN *rises slowly.*)

BLIND MAN

Worship and honour aye to thee,
With all service that can be done!
The king of bliss, loved might he be,
That thus my sight has sent me soon,
And all through thee.
I was as blind as any stone;
But now I see.

(*Procession. A* BURGHER *steps out of the crowd.*)

BURGHER

Hail, blissful babe in Bethleme born!

ALL

Hail!

BURGHER

Ransomer of sinners all!

ALL

Hail!

BURGHER
He that shaped both even and morn!

ALL
Hail!

BURGHER
Welcome of us shall on thee fall!

ALL
Hail!

BURGHER
Royal Jew!

ALL
Hail!

BURGHER
Comely corse, that we thee call
With mirth still new

ALL
Hail!

BURGHER
Sun aye shining with bright beams!

ALL
Hail!

BURGHER
Lamp of life that ne'er goes out!

ALL
Hail!

BURGHER
Lucid lanterns' lovely gleams

ALL
Hail!

BURGHER
Salver of our sores so stout!
We welcome thee!

ALL
Hail!

BURGHER
And welcome of all about
To our city!

ALL
Hail!

(Music and procession. The BAND *returns to its place on the stage.*
As the music ends JUDAS *jumps down from the bridge on to the*
stage. JUDAS *prowls up and down addressing the audience.)*

JUDAS
Unjustly injured, I Judas, by Jesus, that Jew!
Bursar was I, balancing t'brethren's budgeting book.
To temptations I tumbled, to tell the tale true.
And a tenth of each total the treasurer took.

At Bethany betimes my bale did begin,
When Mary brought balm in a beauteous box
In t'best of all alabaster was t'balm brought in
And she lollopeth the lot on yon lotterell's locks!

'What waste', wailed I then, 'that woman hath
wrought!
Seeing spikenard so slopped, sir, seres my soul sore.
What blessing to t'burdened that balm might have
bought.
Its 300 pence price provide plenty for t'poor.
Think of folk famished and feeble that fortune would
feed.

Judge ye, gentills all, what that Jesus did jaw –

'Judas, the needy shall never not need,
But among ye may I move not a moon more.'

99

The poor's plight pricked me not, to play no pretence.
What pricked me and pined me was t'loss of my pence.

The cause which that cursed Christ to cumbrance shall
                      come
And foiled of my fiddle full fast will I flit,
Sell that sauntering sawterell for that selfsame sum
And thirty pence pocket from Pontius Pilate.

(*Exit* JUDAS *to booing.*
During the music the THREE WOMEN *set the table for the Last
Supper.*)

BAND
On Holy Wednesday and all in the morning.
Judas betrayed our Heavenly King.
And was not this a woeful thing.
And sweet Jesus they call him by name.

For thirty silver pieces they sold our saviour.
And Peter thrice denied our Heavenly King.
And was not this a woeful thing.
And sweet Jesus they call him by name.

The Last Supper

JESUS *enters the pit and the* DISCIPLES *form a circle.*

JESUS
Peace be both by day and night
Unto this house, and to all that's here.
Here will I hold, as I have hight,
The feast of Pasch with friends full dear.
Therefore array you all in row;
Myself shall part it you between.

Wherefore I will that ye
Eat thereof every one;
The remnant parted shall be
To the poor that purveys none.

Marcell, my own disciple dear,
Do bring us water here in haste.

(MARCELLUS *brings a bowl of water and a towel.*)

MARCELLUS
Master, it's already here,
And here a towel clean to taste.

JESUS
Come forth with me together here;
My words shall not be wrought in waste.
Set your feet forth; let's see.
They shall be washen soon.

PETER
Ah, Lord by the leave of thee,
That deed shall not be done.
Never I shall make my members meet
Nor see service, Lord, from thee.

JESUS
Peter, unless thou let me wash thy feet
Thou gets no part in bliss with me.

PETER
Ah mercy, Lord and master sweet!
Out of that bliss that I not be,
Wash on, my Lord, till all be wet,
Both head and hand, I beseech thee.

(*Music.* JESUS *takes the towel from* MARCELLUS *and goes anticlockwise round the circle of* DISCIPLES, *and washes the feet of each one.* JESUS *forgets* MARCELLUS *who reminds him with a little cough.* JESUS *washes the feet of* MARCELLUS *and the other* DISCIPLES *laugh.*

JESUS *then crosses to the table laid for the Last Supper and takes up his position behind his place at the centre of the table. The* DISCIPLES *follow to their positions with* JUDAS *at the end stage. The* DISCIPLES *sit.* MARCELLUS *sets bread and wine on the table in front of* JESUS.

101

JESUS *picks up the bread and breaks it in half.)*

JESUS
This bread that I do bless and break
It is my corse no common crust.
This beaker's t'blood shed for thy sake
And sup of it ilk man you must.

(JESUS *goes behind the disciples with bread and wine. He tears off a piece of bread for each disciple, and the disciples pass on the goblet of wine from one to another.)*

One who hath broke bread with me
Shall me into cumbrance cast.
See where I serve this sop — tis he!

(JESUS *hands bread to* JUDAS.)

(*To* JUDAS)
What thou must do, do thou full fast.

(*The* DISCIPLES *murmur anxiously amoung themselves and cast suspicious glances towards* JUDAS *who rises and moves into the pit.*)

JUDAS
Now is it time for me to gang,
For here begins annoy all new.
My fellows mummels them among,
That I should all this bargain brew.
And certes they shall not weep it wrong;
To the prince of priests I shall pursue,
And they shall learn him other ere long,
That all his saws sore shall him rue.
I know where he removes
With his fellows ilk one;
I shall tell to the Jews,
And tite he shall be ta'en.

(*Exit* JUDAS.)

JESUS

(*To* DISCIPLES)

> I warn you now, my friends so free;
> See to these sayings that I say.
> The fiend is wroth with you and me,
> And will you mar, if that he may.
> But Peter, I have prayed for thee,
> So that thou shalt not fear his affray;
> And comfort thou this company
> And guide them, when I am gone away.

PETER

> Ah, Lord, where thou wilt stay
> I shall stay in that stead,
> And with thee make my way
> Evermore, alive or dead.

ANDREW

> No worldly dread shall me withdraw,
> But I shall with thee live and die.

JOHN

> Certes, so shall we all on row,
> Else mickle woe were we worthy.

(*The* DISCIPLES *beat with their hands on the table to show their agreement.*)

JESUS

(*To* PETER)

> Peter, I say to you this saw,
> Which you shall find no fantasy.
> This very night ere the cock crow,
> Shalt thou three times my name deny,
> And say ye knew me never,
> Nor company of mine.

PETER

> Alas, lord, I would liever
> Be put to endless pine.

(Music (drums). DISCIPLES *all rise.*
PILATE *enters on the bridge above the stage. When he reaches centre the drums stop.* PERCULA *enters on the bridge, meets* PILATE *centre. Exeunt* DISCIPLES *from the table.)*

Pilate and Percula

PILATE

Lo, Pilate am I, proved prince of great pride,
I was put into Pontius, the people to press;
And then Caesar himself, with senators by side,
Remitted me to these realms, all ranks to redress.

PERCULA

I am Dame Precious Percula, of princesses the prize,
Wife to Sir Pilate here, prince without peer.
All well of all womanhood am I, witty and wise
Conceive now my countenance so comely and clear.

PILATE

Now say may ye safely; I will certify the same.

PERCULA

Gracious lord, gramercy; your good word is gain.

PILATE

Yet to comfort my corse, I must kiss you, madame.

PERCULA

To fulfil your forward, my fair lord, I am fain.

PILATE

How, how, fellows! Now in faith I am fain
Of these lips that so lovely are lapped.

(PILATE *kisses* PERCULA.)

In bed 'tis full blithe to remain.

PERCULA

Yea, sir; it needs must be plain.

PILATE

All ladies, we covet them both to be kissed and be
clapped.

(Enter CAYPHAS *followed by* ANNAS *on to the stage below*
PILATE *and* PERCULA.*)*

CAYPHAS

My liberal lord, O leader of laws
I beseech you, my sovereign, assent to my saws –

PERCULA

How now! Hearken, jawing and jangling of Jews!
Why, begone, whoreson boy, when I bid thee;
Away, cursed carl; haste thee and hide thee!

PILATE

Do mend you, madame, and your mood be amending
For meseems it were fitting to hear what he says.

ANNAS

Sir, for to certify the sooth in your sight
To you as our sovereign seemly we seek.

PILATE

Why, is there some mischief that musters his might?

ANNAS

Yea, sir; there is a rank swain
Whose rule is not right
For he teaches folk him for to call
Great God's son; thus grieves he us all.

CAYPHAS

To us, sir, his law is full loth.

PILATE

Beware that ye wax not too wroth.

CAYPHAS

Sir, without this abating, there hangs as I hope
A man hilt full of ire, for hasty he is.

PILATE

What comes he for?

CAYPHAS

I ken him not, but he is clad in a cape.
He comes with a keen face, uncomely to kiss.

PILATE

Go get him, that his grief we may straitly grope
So no open language be going amiss.

ANNAS

(*To* JUDAS)

Come on lively now to my lords, if ye list for to leap,
But utter so thy language that thou bar not their bliss.

(*Enter* JUDAS.)

JUDAS

Sir Pilate most potent a plea I pursue
That Jesus, that Jew, I would sell unto you.

PILATE

What hightest thou?

JUDAS

Judas Scariot.

PILATE

Howgates bought shall he be? Bring forth thy bargain.

JUDAS

But for a little amends to bear hence again.

PILATE

Nay, what shall we pay?

JUDAS

Sir, thirty pence, flat; no more then.

(*Music.* PILATE *takes out a bag of coins and drops them one by one to the stage below.* JUDAS *scrabbles about collecting them as they fall. On the final note of the music* PILATE *throws down a handful of coins which* JUDAS *catches in his outstretched robe.*)

I shall teach you a token him quick for to take.
Where he is ringed in the throng; my word I will keep

(JUDAS *leaves the stage for the pit.*)

PILATE

(*Calling after* JUDAS)
We know him not.

(JUDAS *stops and calls up to* PILATE *on the bridge.*)

JUDAS

Take care then that caitiff to catch
Whom there I shall kiss

(*Exit* JUDAS.)

PILATE

(*To* CAYPHAS *and* ANNAS)
Now farewell, and walk on your way.

(*To* PERCULA *putting his arm round her shoulder*)
I command thee, come near;
I will to my couch.
Have me in your hands handily,
    and heave me from here.

(PILATE *and* PERCULA *begin their exit,* PILATE *leaning heavily on his wife.*)

PERCULA

Ah, sir, ye weigh well.

PILATE

Yea, I have wet me with wine.
Look that no man or minion of mine
With no noise may come nigh me or near.

(*Exeunt* PILATE *and* PERCULA. *Music. During music* JESUS *enters and kneels among the standing audience in the pit. Music stops.*)

The Agony and the Betrayal

JESUS

(Kneeling)

Thou, Father, that all formed has with food for to fill,
I feel by my feardness my flesh would full fain
Be turned from this torment and taken thee until,
For mazed is my manhood in mood and in main.

But if thee see soothly that thy son still
Withouten surfeit of sin thus sakless be slain.
Be it worthy wrought even at thy own will,
For, Father, at thy bidding am I buxum and bayne...
Salver of all sore, some succour me send.
The Passion they purpose to put me upon
My flesh is full feared and fain would defend.
At Thy will be it wrought and right worthily won.
Have mind of my manhood, my mood for to mend.
Some comfort I crave in this case.
And Father, I shall death taste
I will it not defend;
Yet if thy will be
Spare me a space.

(An ANGEL appears at the upper level.)

ANGEL

Unto thee maker unmade that most is of might
Be loving ay lasting in light that is lent.
Thy Father that in heaven is most, He upon height,
Thy sorrows for to sober, to thee has me sent.
For deeds that man has thy death shall be dight,
And thou with torments be toiled, but take now intent.

Thy bale shall be for the best.
Through that shall man's sin be amend;
Then shall thou withouten any end
Reign in thy royalty full of rest.

(The ANGEL disappears.)

JESUS

Now in my flesh feared be, Father, I am fain
That mine anguish and my noyes are near at an end.

(JESUS *rises.*)

Unto my disciples go will I again
Kindly to comfort them that mazed is in their mind.

(JESUS *moves to* PETER.)

Now will this hour be nighing full near
That'll certify all the sooth that I've said.

(*Enter* JUDAS.)

JUDAS

All hail, Master, in faith, and fellows all here.
With great, gracious greeting on t'ground be arrayed.
I would ask you a kiss, Master, if your will were,
For all my love and my liking wholly on you is laid.

JESUS

Full heartily, Judas, have it even here.

(JUDAS *embraces* JESUS.)

For with this kiss is Man's Son betrayed.

(*Four* KNIGHTS *surround* JESUS *from all sides.* PETER *moves to defend* JESUS.)

KNIGHT 1

Ha! stand, traitor. I tell thee for ta'en.

(*A brilliant light shines from the body of* JESUS.)

KNIGHT 3

Alas! we are lost for gleam of this light.

JESUS

Say ye here, whom seek ye? Do tell me; let's see.

KNIGHT 4

One Jesus of Nazareth; I think that name right.

JESUS

Behold ye all hitherward. Lo, here; I am he.

KNIGHT 1

Stand, dastard. So dreadful thy death shall be dight.
I'll be no more abashed thy shining to see.

KNIGHT 3

Ah, out! I am amazed almost in main and in might.

KNIGHT 2

And I fear, by my faith, and fain would I flee;
For such a sight have I not seen.

KNIGHT 3

This gleam, it gleamed so light,
I saw ne'er such a sight.
Me marvel much what it may mean.

JESUS

Come, whom seek ye assembled, yet I say?

KNIGHT 1

One Jesus of Naz'reth; him would we nigh now.

JESUS

And I am he soothly, And that shall I say.

(MALCUS *moves towards* JESUS.)

MALCUS

For that shalt thou die, dastard, Since it is thou.

PETER

And I shall try by my faith thee for to flay.
Here with a lash, lurdan, I shall thee allow.

(PETER *raises a putty knife and cuts off* MALCUS's *ear.*
MALCUS *claps his hand to his ear and falls to his knees.*)

MALCUS

Ah, behold what the dastard hath done!

PETER

Nay, traitor, but truly I shall trap thee, I trow.

JESUS

Peace, Peter, I bid thee;
Fash thee no further, nor frame thee to fight
If my will were, as thou well wit,
I might have power in great plenty
Of angels full many to muster my might.
So put thy sword in its sheath, and haste not to hit.
He that smites with sword, with sword shall be smit.

(*To* MALCUS)

Thou man thus in dread and doefully dight,
Come here to me safely and be salved of thy pain.
In the name of my Father that in heaven is most in
                                        height,
Of thy hurts be thou whole in hide and in bone,
As this virtue in thy veins shall avail.

(JESUS *restores* MALCUS'S *ear.* MALCUS *touches it in wonder.*)

MALCUS

What? All hail! I believe that I be whole!
Now beshrew him this time that gives tale
To touch thee for thy travail.

(MALCUS *kisses the robe of* JESUS.
KNIGHT 1 *moves towards* JESUS *with a noose.* KNIGHT 3 *moves in from the other side.*)

KNIGHT 1

Do, fellows, by your faith, let us hang on all here.
For I have on this hind firm hold as I can.

KNIGHT 2

(*Moving in to the right of* JESUS)

And I have a lock on him now. How, fellows, draw
                                        near.

(*They seize* JESUS.)

KNIGHT 3

Yea, by the bones that him bare this jest shall he ban.

(KNIGHT 4 *clears a way through the audience in the pit, and* KNIGHTS *begin to drag* JESUS *away.*)

JESUS

Even like a thief heinously hurl ye me here.
I taught in your Temple; why took ye me not then?
Now has darkness on earth all his power.

(*The bright light issuing from the body of* JESUS *disappears. Music.* KNIGHTS *drag* JESUS *round the pit and off.*)

The Palace of the High Priest, Cayphas

Enter CAYPHAS *on the stage.*

CAYPHAS

With witchcraft he fares withal;
Sirs, that same shall ye see full soon.
Our knights, all forth they went
To take him and betray;
By this I hold him spent;
He cannot wend away.

(*Enter* ANNAS *bearing a large goblet of wine.*)

ANNAS

Would ye, sir, take your rest –
The day is come at hand –
And with wine slake your thirst?
Then durst I well warrant
Ye should have tidings soon
Of the knights that are gone,
And how they yet have done,
To trap and take him anon.
Now put all thought away,
And let your matters rest.

112

CAYPHAS

(Taking the goblet from ANNAS*)*

> I will do as ye say;
> Do give us wine of the best.
> For be we once well wet,
> The better will we rest.

ANNAS

> My lord, here is wine that will make you to wink;
> It is liquor full delicious, my lord, if you like.
> Wherefore I deam deeply a draught that ye drink,
> For in this country that we know I vow is none like.
> Therefore we counsel you
> This cup savoury for to kiss.

CAYPHAS

(Belching)

> Come now daintily, and dress me on t'dais,
> And handily heap on me happing,
> And warn all wights to be in peace,
> For I am laid late unto napping.

ANNAS

> My lord, with your leave,
> If it like you, I pass.

CAYPHAS

(To audience)

> Adieu be unto you,
> As the manner has.

(Exit CAYPHAS *and* ANNAS. *Music (drums).)*

Peter denies Jesus

Enter WOMAN *who faces* KNIGHTS *holding* JESUS. PETER *stands opposite.*

WOMAN

> Sir knights, do keep this boy so bound,
> For I will go wit what it may mean,

Why that yon wight was following found
Early and late, morning and even.
He will come near, he will not let;
He is a spy, I warrant, full bold.

KNIGHT 3
It seems by his semblance he'd sooner be set
By the fervent fire, to flee from the cold.

WOMAN
Yea, but ye wist as well as I
What wonders that this wight has wrought;
And for his master's sorcery
Full fiercely should his death be bought.

KNIGHT 1
Dame, we have him now at will
That we have long time sought;
If others go by us still,
For them we have no thought.

WOMAN
It were great scorn if he should 'scape,
Without he had reason and skill;
He looketh lurking like an ape;
I think in haste to take him still.
Thou caitiff, what moves thee to stand
So stable and still in thy thought?
Thou has wrought mickle wrong in land,
And wonderful works hast thou wrought.
Wait now! He looks like a brock,
Were he in a band bound for to bait;
Or else like an owl on a stock,
Full privily his prey for to wait.

PETER
Woman, thy words and thy wind do not waste.
Of his company never was I kenned.

Though has mismarked me, truly me trust;
Wherefore of thy miss do thou mend.

WOMAN

Then hen heart avow all ye averred was amiss
When ye said that yon sawterell shall save us from sin
And gainsay that that gadling God's given son is
Who walketh the world all wights' worship to win.

PETER

I will consent to your saws; what should I say more?
For women are crabbed; that comes of their kind.
But I say as I first said, I ne'er saw him e'er.
But as a friend of your fellowship shall ye me aye find.

(WOMAN *leads* MALCUS *from the crowd to before the* KNIGHTS
and JESUS.)

WOMAN

Say how this sawterell swiped off thine ear.

MALCUS

Yea, sirs, this sawterell swiped off my ear.

WOMAN

This lurdan lashed out and lopped off thy lug.

MALCUS

This lurdan lashed out and lopped off my lug.

WOMAN

How that harlot full hastily made it all whole.

MALCUS

This Jesu here hastily made it all whole.

PETER

I was never with him in work that he wrought,
In word nor work, in will nor in deed.
I know none that ye have hither brought,
In no court of this kith, if I should right rede.

(A cock crows.)

JESUS
Peter, Peter, thus said I ere,
When you said you would abide with me
In weal and in woe, in sorrow and care,
Whilst I should thrice forsaken be.

PETER
Alas the while that I came here,
Or e'er denied my Lord apart.
The look of his fair face so clear
With full sad sorrow shears my heart.

(PETER *screams. Music. Exeunt four* KNIGHTS *and* JESUS *from their 'cart' and enter on the stage.)*

Jesus Examined by Cayphas

Enter CAYPHAS *and* ANNAS *on the stage.*

CAYPHAS
If thou be Christ, God's son, tell it to us two.

JESUS
Sir, thou sayest it thyself, and soothly I say,
That I shall go to my father as I came fro,
And dwell with him joyful in weal alway.

CAYPHAS
Why, fie on thee, traitor, untrue!
The father hast thou foully defamed.

(To audience)

Now need we no notices new;
Himself with his saws he has shamed.

ANNAS
Now needs neither witness nor counsel to call,
But take his saws as he says them in the same stead,

He slanders the Godhead and so grieves us all,
Wherefore well worthy is he to be dead.
And therefore, sir, tell him the truth.

CAYPHAS

Surely, so I shall
Hearest thou not, harlot? I'll hap on thy head.
Answer here directly to great and to small,
And reach us out rapidly some reason, I rede.

JESUS

My reasons are not to rehearse
Nor they that might help me are not here now.

ANNAS

Nay, lad, if ye list to make verse,
Priest prattles prettier poetry than thou.

JESUS

Sir, if I say thee sooth, thou shalt not assent,
But hinder, or haste me to hang.
I preached where people were most present,
And no point in privity to old nor young.
And also in your Temple I told my intent;
Ye might have taken me then for my telling,
Much better than bring me with brands unburnt,
Thus to noy me by night, and also for nothing.

CAYPHAS

For nothing! Losel, thou liest.
Thy words and thy works a vengeance will bring.

JESUS

Sir, since thou with wrong so turnest me awry,
Go ask them that heard of my speaking.

CAYPHAS

Go dress you and ding you him down,
And deafen us no more with his deeds.

(KNIGHT 1 *stands in front of* JESUS *and pulls hard on the rope round his neck, dragging him with one jerk to the ground.* KNIGHTS *2, 3, 4, close round* JESUS *and raise their hammer, wrench, and pliers, above their heads as if to strike* JESUS. *They freeze in that position, forming a tableau of the 'buffeting'.* CAYPHAS *and* ANNAS *turn away.*)

> Go, tell to Sir Pilate our plaints all plain,
> And say, this lad with his lying has our laws lorn;
> And say, this same day must he be slain,
> Because of the Sabbath which is in the morn;
> And say that we come ourselves for certain,
> For to further the affair. Now fare ye before.

(KNIGHTS *emerge from the frozen tableau, and raise* JESUS *from the ground. They begin to drag him away.*)

ANNAS
Sir, your fair fellowship we commend to the fiend.

(*Exit* ANNAS.)

CAYPHAS
Go on, now; dance forth in the devil's way.

(*Exit* CAYPHAS.
KNIGHTS *drag* JESUS *away.*
Music. During the music JUDAS *emerges from the crowd carrying a bag of money.*)

The Remorse of Judas

JUDAS
(*To audience*)

> Alas, for woe that I was wrought,
> Ere ever I came by kind or kin.
> I ban the bones that forth me brought;
> Woe worth the womb that I bred in,
>   So may I bid.
> For I so falsely did to him
> That unto me great kindness did.

118

The purse with his expense about I bore;
There was none trusted so well as I.
Than me he trusted no man more,
And I betrayed him traitorly
    With lies all vain.
Blameless I sold his body
Unto his foes for to be slain.
To slay my sovereign assented I,
And told them the time of his taking.
Shameless myself thus ruined I,
So soon to assent to his slaying.
Now wist I how he might pass that pain. . .
To look how best that boon might be

(Enter PILATE *on the bridge above the stage.*
Enter CAYPHAS *and* ANNAS *on the stage.)*

To priests and Sir Pilate I will again,
To save him, that he might pass free.
    That were my will.
Lords, wealth and worship with you be.

PILATE

What tidings, Judas, tellest thou still?

JUDAS

My tidings are painful, I tell you,
Sir Pilate, and therefore I pray,
My master that I did sell you,
Good lord, let him wend his way.

CAYPHAS

Nay, needs must, Judas, that we deny.
What mind or matter has moved thee thus?

JUDAS

Sir, I have sinned full grievously,
Betrayed that righteous blood Jesus
    And master mine.

CAYPHAS

Fair sir, what is that to us?
The peril and the plight are thine.
Thine is the wrong, and thou has wrought it;
Thou told us full truly to take him;
And ours is the bargain, for we bought it.
Lo, we all assent for to slay him.

JUDAS

Alas, that may I rue full ill,
If ye assent him for to slay.

PILATE

These words that thou names nought needs it.
Thou unhanged harlot, hark what I say.
Spare of thy speaking, for nought speeds it;
Or walk out at the door, in the devil's way.

JUDAS

Why, will ye then not let him pass,
And have of me again your pay?

(JUDAS *holds up the bag of money to* PILATE.)

PILATE

I tell thee, traitor, that I will not.

JUDAS

Then am I lorn this day, alas,
    Both bone and blood.
Alas the while, so may I say,
That ever I assent to spill his blood.
To save his blood see, sirs, I pray you,

(JUDAS *again holds up the bag of money to* PILATE.)

And take you there your payment whole.
Spare for to spill him, now I pray you,
Else brew ye me full mickle dole.

PILATE

Now hearest thou me, Judas, thou shalt take it again;
We will it not; what the devil art thou?
When thou sought us, thou wast full fain
Of this money; what ails thee now
    For to repent?

(*Exit* PILATE.)

JUDAS

That which you took of me, take you it there!

(JUDAS *throws down the bag of money at his feet.*)

Therewith your mastery make you among,
And claim it you clean.
I loathe all my life, so live I too long;
My treacherous turn torments me with pain.
Since so my treason I have taken unto me,
I need ask no mercy, for none shall I get.
Therefore in haste myself shall I fordo me.
Alas the hard while that I ever met yet.
To slay myself now will I speed,
For sadly have I served too ill.
    So welaway.
That ever I was in wit or will,
That trusty true one to betray.
Alas, who may I move unto?
No other counsel now I need;
Myself in haste I shall fordo,
And take me now unto my death.

(*Exit* JUDAS *through the crowd/audience, drawn by the figure of*
DEATH.

CAYPHAS *and* ANNAS *meet in the centre of the stage over the bag
of money.*)

CAYPHAS

Come then now, Sir Annas, let us see what you say
As touching this money that here we have,

That Judas in wrath has waved away
And cast to us crabbedly, that cursed knave.
How say ye thereby?

ANNAS

(*Picking up the bag of money*)
Sir, since he it slung, we shall it save.

CAYPHAS

Quick, carry it to our treasury.

(*Music. Exeunt* CAYPHAS *and* ANNAS *in opposite directions. Song:*)

BAND

Look up, look up,
The lamb shall lead the way,
Look up, look up,
The dogs behowl the day.
And they shall bite,
Full bellied in their spite.
What care have they,
To take the lamb away.

Look up, look up.
The hand devides the gloom.
Look up, look up.
The prophet or the doom,
And should we die,
On whose word can we rely.
The truth to see,
Death or eternity.

Look up, look up,
The shepherd takes his place.
Look up, look up.
A mother hides her face.
And when we die,
Will there be friends to cry.
What hope have they,

Who turn their heads away.

(Words and music by John Tams.)

(During the song the FOUR KNIGHTS *enter with* JESUS, *and set him down on the steps facing the centre of the stage, at the opposite end of the pit.*
A chair is set centre stage for PILATE.)

The Trial before Pilate and the Judgement of Jesus

PILATE
Speak; and excuse thee, if thou can.

JESUS
Every man has a mouth that made is on mould,
In weal and in woe to wield at his will.
If he govern it goodly, like as God would,
For his spiritual speech he needs not to spill;
And what man shall govern it ill,
Full unhandy and ill shall he hap.
For each tale thou talks us until
You account shall; you cannot escape.

PILATE
Sirs mine,
Ye found, in faith, all his design;
For in this lad no lies can I trap,
Nor no point to put him to pine.

CAYPHAS
Without cause, sir, we come not, this carl to accuse
him;
That will we ye wit, as well as worthy.

PILATE
Now I record well the right; ye will no sooner refuse
him
Till he be driven to his death and doomed to die.
But take him to you thereby,

And like as your law will decide,
Doom ye his body to abide.

ANNAS
O, Sir Pilate without any peer,
Now nay;
Ye wot well (no doubt can appear)
We may not, not all of us here,
Slay no man, to you truth to say.

PILATE
Shall I doom him to death, not deserving in deed?
But I have heard wholly why in heart ye him hate.
He is faultless, in faith, and so God might me speed,
I grant him my good will to gang on his gate.

(PILATE *rises from his chair.*)

CAYPHAS
Not so, sir; for well ye it wot,
To be king he claimeth with crown.
Who so stoutly will step to that state,
You should doom, sir, to be donged down
    And dead.

PILATE
Sir, truly that touches to treason,
And ere I remove he shall rue that reason,
Ere I stalk or stir from this stead.
Sir knights that are comely, take this caitiff in keeping;
Skelp him with scourges and with scathes him scorn;
Wrest him and wring him till for woe he is weeping,
And then bring him before us as he was before.

(PILATE *sits down.*)

KNIGHT 1
He may ban the time that he was born;
Soon shall he be served as ye said us.

KNIGHT 4

Do whop off his weeds that are worn.

KNIGHT 1

(Tearing off JESUS's *robe)*
They are torn off in a trice, take there his trashes.

KNIGHT 4

He is bun fast; now beat on with bitter brashes.
Go on; lep, hear ye, lordings, with lashes.

(KNIGHT 1 *pushes* JESUS *towards* KNIGHT 4 *who punches him.*
KNIGHT 3 *hits* JESUS *and he falls.* KNIGHT 2 *kicks* JESUS.)

KNIGHT 2

For all our annoying, this niggard he naps.

(The KNIGHTS *lift* JESUS *up from the ground.)*

KNIGHT 3

We shall wake him with wind of our whips

KNIGHT 4

Now fling to this flatterer with flaps.

(KNIGHT 1 *gives* JESUS *a savage blow, then* 4, 3, *and* 2 *in turn.*
JESUS *falls again. The* KNIGHTS *lift him up and sit him down on
steps.)*

KNIGHT 3

Now because he a king did him call,
We will kindly him crown with a briar.

(KNIGHT 3 *takes pincers from his belt and with them lifts a crown
of barbed wire, and holds it above the head of* JESUS.)

KNIGHT 4

Yea, but first this purple and pall
And this worthy weed shall he wear.

(KNIGHT 2 *puts the purple robe on* JESUS.)

KNIGHT 1

Now thring to him thrayley with this thick thorn.

KNIGHT 2

Thus we teach him to temper his tales.

WOMAN

(Singing)

> On Sheer Thursday and all in the morning
> They made a crown of thorns for our Heavenly King.
> And was not that a woeful thing
> And sweet Jesus they call him by name.

(KNIGHT 1 *and* KNIGHT 3 *hold the crown of barbed wire with pincers, and lower it on to* JESUS's *head.*)

KNIGHT 2

His brain begins for to bleed.

KNIGHT 1

> Now reach him a rush or a reed
>   So round;
> For his sceptre it serves indeed.

(KNIGHT 4 *gives* KNIGHT 3 *a long screwdriver to put in* JESUS's *hand to serve as a sceptre. Then* KNIGHTS *raise* JESUS *to his feet and salute him mockingly as king.*)

KNIGHT 2

(Kneeling)

> Hail, comely king, that no kingdom has kenned!

KNIGHT 3

(Kneeling)

> Hail, man unmighty wi'out means to mend!

NIGHT 4

(Kneeling)

> Hail, lord wi'out land for to lend.

KNIGHT 1

(Kneeling)

> Hail, freak wi'out force thee to fend.

(*The* KNIGHTS *rise.*)

KNIGHT 3

To Sir Pilate the prince our pride will we praise.

KNIGHT 4

Now wightly let us wend on our ways.

(*Music.* KNIGHTS *push* JESUS *up towards* PILATE.)

KNIGHT 1

(*To* PILATE)

My lord, will ye list to our lays?
Here this boy is you bade us go harry
    With blows.
We are cumbered his corse for to carry.
Many wights on him wonder and worry.
Lo, his flesh, how its beatings it shows.

PILATE

Well, bring him before us.

(KNIGHT 1 *gives* JESUS *a push, so that he staggers nearer to* PILATE.)

                    Ah, he blushes all blue.
I suppose of his saying he'll cease evermore.
Sirs, look here on high and see: ECCE HOMO
Thus bounden and beat and brought you before.
Meseems that it serves him full sore.
                Bring forth Barabbas!

(PILATE *moves closer to* JESUS *and begins to address the crowd.*)

This feast is it fashion a felon to free.
Let each man among you make motion to me
Which churl be chastened in chains you must choose
And which prisoner pardoned by Pilate shall pass.

(PILATE *takes hold of the left arm of* BARABBAS *and raises it.*)

Barabbas or . . .

(PILATE *drops* BARABBAS's *arm and raises* JESUS's *right arm.*)

Jesus? Judge, all ye Jews.

CROWD

Barabbas! Barabbas! Barabbas!

PILATE

And Jesus clept Christ, how crave ye, pray cry.
The prisoner shall pine as the people all please.

CROWD

Crucify! Crucify! Crucify!

(PILATE *moves to meet* BOY *with bowl of water and a towel.*
PILATE *washes his hands, then dries them, and turns. As he turns
the* CROWD *stops shouting.*)

PILATE

Of blameless blood shall I unblemished be.
By Mahound this misdeed shall not mar me.
From Barabbas his bonds now unbend;

(KNIGHTS *undo the rope binding* BARABBAS.)

With grace let him gang his gate
      Where you will.

BARABBAS

Ye worthy men goodly and great,
God increase all your comely estate,
For the grace ye grant me until.

(*Exit* BARABBAS.)

PILATE

Hear the judgement of Jesus, all ye in this stead.
Crucify him on a cross, and on Calvary him kill.
I doom him today to die this same death;
Therefore hang him on hight upon that high hill.
And on either side him I will
That a harlot ye hang in this haste;

Methinks it both reason and skill
That amidst, since his malice is most,
   Ye hang him.
Then him torment, some torture to taste.
More words I will not now waste;
But stay not, to death till ye bring him.

(Music.
KNIGHTS *lead* JESUS *off to get the cross.*
exeunt PILATE, CAYPHAS *and* ANNAS.*)*

The Road to Calvary

KNIGHTS 6 2, 3, 4 *bring on the cross.* KNIGHT 1 *clears a way through the crowd for them.*

KNIGHT 1

Make room, make room and rule now right,
That we may with this wearied wight
Wightely wend on our way
He has napped not in all this night,
And this day shall his death be dight;
Let's see who dares say nay.
Because tomorrow we provide
For our dear Sabbath day,
We will nought amiss be moved.
But mirth in all that ever men may.
We have been busy all this morn
To clothe him and to crown with thorn,
As befits a folly king.
Why, wot thou not as well as I
This carl must unto Calvary
And there on t'cross be done?

(Music. JESUS *lifts the cross, and moves slowly round the pit.*
JESUS *drops the cross, as* JOHN *followed by* MARY MOTHER,
MARY MAGDALENE, *and* MARY SALOME *enter the pit-side.)*

MARY MOTHER

Alas, the time and tide!
I wot the day is come
That once was specified
By Prophet Simeon,
The sword of sorrow, he said, should run
Through this heart subtily.

MARY MAGDALENE

Alas, this is a pitiful sight!
He that was ever lovely and light,
And lord of high and low,
How dolefully now is he dight.
In world is none so woeful wight,
Nor so troubled to know.
They that he mended most,
In deed and word also,
Now have they full great haste
To death him for to draw.

JESUS

Daughters of Jerusalem City,
See, and mourn no more for me,
But think upon this thing.
Turn home to town again,
Since ye have seen this sight;
It is my Father's will,
All that is done and dight.

MARY SALOME

Alas, this is a cursèd case.
He that all heal in his hand has
Shall here be blameless slain.
Ah Lord, give leave to clean thy face . . .

(MARY SALOME *carries a towel to* JESUS. *She wipes his face then stares at the towel.*)

Behold! how he has shewed his grace,
He that is most of main.

This sign shall bear witness
Unto all people plain,
How God's Son here guiltless
Is put to peerless pain.

(KNIGHT 1 *pushes* MARY SALOME *away.*)

KNIGHT 1
Say, whereto bide ye here about,
Ye crones, with screaming and with shout?
What do these stevenings here?

KNIGHT 2
Go home, thou baldhead, with thy clout,
Or, by that lord we love and lout,
Thou shalt abide full dear.

MARY SALOME
This sign shall vengeance call
On you all that are here.

KNIGHT 3
Go, hie thee hence withal,
Or ill hail come thou here.

JOHN
Lady, your weeping grieves me sore.

MARY MOTHER
John, help me now or nevermore,
That I to him might come.

JOHN
My lady, wend we on before,
To Calvary; when we come there,
You shall say what you will.

KNIGHT 1
What a devil is this to say?
How long shall we stand still?
Go, hie you hence away,
In the devil's name, up the hill.

(JESUS *picks up the cross again and continues round the pit. Then he stumbles and stops.*)

KNIGHT 3

Methinks this boy is so forbled,
With this load may he not be led;
He swoons, that dare I swear.

KNIGHT 1

It needs not hard to haul;

KNIGHT 2

I see here comes a carl
Shall help him forth to bear.

(*Enter* SIMON OF CYRENE *approaching the* KNIGHTS.)

KNIGHT 3

That shall we see one soon essay.
Good man, whither is thou away?
You walk as if in wrath.

SIMON

Sir, I have a great journey,
That must be done on this same day,
Or else it may do scathe.

KNIGHT 1

Thou mayest with little pain
Ease thyself and us both.

SIMON

Good sirs, that would I fain,
But to dwell were I loath.

KNIGHT 2

Nay, fair sir, you shall soon be sped.
Lo, here a lad that must be led
For his ill deeds to die.

KNIGHT 4

And he is bruised and all forbled,

That makes us here thus still bested.
We pray thee, sir, thereby,
That thou wilt take this tree,
And bear it to Calvary.

SIMON

I pray you, do your deed,
And let me go my way.
And, sirs, I shall come soon again,
To help this man with all my main,
And even at your own will.

KNIGHT 2

What? Wouldst thou trick us so, and feign?
Let's ding the dastard down,
If he speeds not thereto.

SIMON

Sure, sir, that was not wisely wrought,
To beat me, though I trespassed nought,
Either in word or deed.

KNIGHT 1

Upon his back it shall be brought
To bear it, whether he will or not.
What the devil! Whom should we dread?
Go, take it up. Be alive,
And bear it with good speed.

(SIMON *and* JESUS *look at one another.*)

SIMON

It helps not here to strive;
Bear it then must I need.
And therefore, sirs, as ye have said . . .

(SIMON *helps* JESUS *to his feet, then lifts the cross.*)

To bear this cross I hold me glad
Right as ye would it were.

KNIGHT 3

If any ask after us,
Call them to Calvary.

(Music. SIMON *circles the pit once carrying the cross, followed by*
KNIGHTS *and* JESUS.
SIMON *puts down the cross and exits.*
KNIGHTS *put the cross into position facing upstage with its foot*
downstage.
KNIGHT 4 *three bricks, throws one to* KNIGHT 2 *who places it*
under the foot of the cross. KNIGHT 3 *puts a brick under the right*
arm of the cross, and KNIGHT 4 *under the left arm.)*

The Crucifixion

KNIGHT 1

Sir knights, take heed and hither hie
This fastenin' up falls to us four.
Ye wot yourselves as well as I
How lords and leaders of our law
Have given doom this dolt'll die.

*(*KNIGHT 4 *who, throughout the scene, is the eagerest to get on*
with the job goes to the toolbags for a length of rope.)

KNIGHT 2

Ay we heard all that afore
But now we're come to Calvary

*(*KNIGHT 2 *looks at* KNIGHT 3, *who is something of the butt of the*
group.)

Muck in 'n' moan no more.

KNIGHT 3

Moaning, nay I know I'm not
So, sirs, let all make speed.

*(*KNIGHT 4 *throws the end of the length of rope to the right arm of*
the cross.)

KNIGHT 4

Just you work out whose job is what
And we shall do this deed.

(KNIGHT 4 *moves to the toolbags for a second length of rope.*)

KNIGHT 1

(Moving to toolbags)
We must start, sirs and that right soon
If we shall any wages win.

KNIGHT 2

(Moving to toolbags)
He must be dead, needs must, by noon.

KNIGHT 3

(Moving to toolbags)
Then it is good time that we begin.

KNIGHT 4

(Taking the length of rope)
Let's ding him down! Then he is done.
He shall not daunt us with his din.

KNIGHT 1

T'lad needs lesson, learn him one
wi' care to him and all his kin.

KNIGHT 2

This lad his life shall loss
In the worst of woeful ways.

KNIGHT 3

That means, put him up on t'cross.

(KNIGHTS 1, 2, 4 *stare at* KNIGHT 3.)

KNIGHT 4

'ark at what the smart lad says.

KNIGHT 1

Then to this work us must tek heed,
So that our working be not wrong.

KNIGHT 2

None other note to name is need
But let us haste him for to hang.

KNIGHT 3

And I've gone for gear, good speed
Both hammers and nails large an' long.

KNIGHT 4

Then may we boldly do this deed
Come on, let's kill this traitor strong.

KNIGHT 1

This lad's like not to be t'last
We'll rivet to t'rough rood.

KNIGHT 2

And we'll fasten him full fast
And wedge this wight to t'wood.

KNIGHT 3

Since ilka thing is right arrayed
The wiselier now work may we.

KNIGHT 4

The cross on t'ground is goodly spread
And bored even as it ought to be.

KNIGHT 1

Look that the lad on length be laid,
And made be tied unto this tree.

KNIGHT 2

For all his brag he shall be brayed:

(Turning to crowd/audience)

Stay stood there and you shall see.

KNIGHT 3

(To JESUS*)*

Thou cursèd cur, come forth
Thy comfort soon shall cool.

KNIGHT 4

(*To* JESUS)

Win the wages thou art worth.

KNIGHT 1

(*To* JESUS)

Walk on! Now work we well!

JESUS

Almighty God, my Father free
Let these matters be marked in mind
Thou bade that I should buxsome be
For Adam's plight I must be pined.
Here to death I do pledge me
Saving mankind that has sinned
And sovereignly beseech I thee
That they through me may favour find.
And from the fiend them fend,
So that their souls be safe,
In wealth wi'out'en end;
I care nought else to crave.

(JESUS *walks towards the cross.*)

KNIGHT 1

Hey, hark, sir knights, for Mahound's blood!
Of Adam's kind is all his thought.

KNIGHT 2

This warlock waxes worse than wode!
This doleful death ne dreadeth he nought.

KNIGHT 3

Thou should have mind with main and mood
Of wicked works that thou did'st do.

KNIGHT 4

Had that wight had wit he would
Have ceased off saws he swore was true.

KNIGHT 1

(*Holding up saw from toolbag*)
>These saws shall rue him sore
>For all his sauntering, soon.

KNIGHT 2

>Ill speed them that him spare
>Till he to death be done!

KNIGHT 3

(*To* JESUS)
>Have done, belive boy and make thee boun
>And bend thy back unto this tree.

(JESUS *unfastens his purple robe, and lets it fall to the ground. He lies down on the cross, and stretches out his arms in position.*)

KNIGHT 4

>Behold, himself has laid him down
>In length and breadth as he should be.

KNIGHT 1

>This traitor here tainted of treason
>Go fast and fetter him then, ye three;
>And since he claims a kingdom's crown
>Even as a king here hang shall he.

KNIGHT 2

(*Taking* JESUS's *right hand*)
>Now, certes, I shall not cease
>Or his right hand be fast.

KNIGHT 3

(*Taking* JESUS's *left hand*)
>The left hand then's my piece
>Let see who bears him best.

KNIGHT 4

(*Going to* JESUS's *feet*)
>His limbs on length shall I lead
>And even unto the bore them bring.

KNIGHT 1

(*Going to* JESUS's *head*)

> Unto his head I shall take heed
> And with mine hand help him to hang.

KNIGHT 2

> Now since we four shall do this deed
> And meddle with this unthrifty thing
> Let no man spare for special speed
> Till we have made ending.

KNIGHT 3

> This forward may not fail
> Now we are right arrayed.

KNIGHT 4

> This boy here in our bail
> Shall bide full bitter braid.

(KNIGHTS 2 *and* 3 *tie* JESUS's *hands to cross.*)

KNIGHT 1

> Sir knights, say here . . . how work we now?

KNIGHT 2

> Why sure I hope I hold this hand.

KNIGHT 3

> And to the bore I have it brought
> Full buxsomely withouten band . . .

KNIGHT 1

> Strike on then. Hard. For him thee bought.

KNIGHT 2

(*Holding up a large nail*)

> Yes, here is a stub will stiffly stand;

(KNIGHT 2 *throws the nail to* KNIGHT 3 *who catches it.*)

> Through bones and sinews it shall be sought.

(KNIGHT 3 *hammers the nail into* JESUS's *left hand.* JESUS *cries out with pain, flinging his right arm into the air.* KNIGHT 2 *grasps* JESUS's *right arm, and stretches it along the arm of the cross to secure it.)*

This work is well, I will warrant.

(KNIGHT 1 *crosses to examine the work.)*

KNIGHT 1
Say, sir, how do we there?
This bargain will we win.

KNIGHT 3
It fails a foot or more
The sinews are so gone in.

KNIGHT 4
I think that mark amiss be bored.

KNIGHT 2
Then must he bide in bitter bale.

KNIGHT 3
In faith it was o'er scantly scored
That makes it foully for to fail.

KNIGHT 1
Why crack ye so? Fast on a cord
And tug him to, by top and tail.

(KNIGHT 2 *ties a rope to the wrist of* JESUS. KNIGHTS 2 *and* 4 *haul on the rope, stretching the arm until it reaches the bore.)*

KNIGHT 3
Yea, thou command us, lightly as a lord:
Come help to haul him, with ill hail!

KNIGHT 1
Now certes that I shall do –
Full snelly, like a snail.

(KNIGHT 1 *makes no attempt to move.)*

KNIGHT 3
(Hammering a nail into JESUS's *right hand)*
> And I shall 'tach him to,
> Full nimbly with a nail.
> This work will hold that dare I heet
> For now are fest fast both his hands.

KNIGHT 4
Go we all four then to his feet
So shall our space be speedily spent.

KNIGHT 2
Let's see what jest his bale might beet.
Thereto my back now would I bend.

KNIGHT 4
(Examining the bore at the foot of the cross)
> Oh! This work is all unmeet
> This boring must all be amend.

KNIGHT 1
Ah, peace man, for Mahoun!
Let no man know what wonder
A rope shall rug him down
If all his sinews go asunder.

KNIGHT 2
That cord full kindly can I knit
The comfort of this carl to cool.

KNIGHT 1
Fest on then fast that all be fit;
It is no force how fell he feel.

*(*KNIGHTS 2 *and* 4 *move to the foot of the cross and haul on the ropes to stretch* JESUS's *legs so that his feet meet the bore.)*

KNIGHT 2
Lug on ye both a little yet.

KNIGHT 3
I shall not cease, as I have zeal.

KNIGHT 4
And I shall fond him for to hit.

KNIGHT 2
Oh! Hail!

KNIGHT 4
Ho now! I hold it well.

KNIGHT 1
Have done, drive in that nail,
So that no fault be found.

(KNIGHT 3 *hammers a nail through* JESUS'S *feet.* KNIGHT 1 *moves down to help him.*)

KNIGHT 4
This working would not fail,
If four bulls were bound.

KNIGHT 1
These cords have evil increased his pains
Ere he were till the borings brought.

KNIGHT 2
(*Taking a closer look at the nails*)
Yea, asunder are both sinews and veins
On ilka side, so have we sought.

KNIGHT 3
Now all his gauds nothing him gains;
His sauntering shall with bale be bought.

KNIGHT 4
I will go say to our sovereigns
Of all these works how we have wrought.

(KNIGHTS 3 *and* 4 *begin to move away.*)

KNIGHT 1
Nay, sirs, another thing
Falls first to you and me:

They bade we should him hang
On height that men might see.

(KNIGHTS 3 *and* 4 *stop. They look at 'the height' (the stage) and at* JESUS *securely fastened to the cross.*)

KNIGHT 2
We wot well so their words were;
But, sir, that deed will do us dear.

KNIGHT 1
It may not mend to moot it more;
This harlot must be hangèd here.

KNIGHT 2
(Inspecting the site for the raising of the cross)
The mortice is made fit therefore.

KNIGHT 3
Fest on your fingers then, all here.

(KNIGHT 3 *throws rope up to* KNIGHT 2. KNIGHT 4 *takes right arm of cross.* KNIGHT 3 *takes left arm. They try to lift the cross. They let it down.*)

KNIGHT 4
I ween it will never come there;
We four'll not raise it right this year.

KNIGHT 1
Say, man, why carp'st thou so?
Thy lifting was but light.

KNIGHT 2
He means there must be more
To heave him up on height.

KNIGHT 3
Now, sirs, I hope it shall not need
More company to cart t'cross there.
Methinks we four should do this deed.
Shrew me if I my wages share.

143

KNIGHT 1

It must be done, wi'out'en dread.
No more! But look ye be ready,

(KNIGHT 1 *goes to left arm of cross,* KNIGHT 3 *to right.*)

And this part shall I lift and lead;
On length he shall no longer lie.
Therefore now make ye boun:
Let's bear him to yon hill.

KNIGHT 4

(Going to foot of cross)
Then will I bear here down,
And tent his toes I will.

KNIGHT 2

This cross'll come out all cock-eyed,
This lad here's like to let it slip.

KNIGHT 3

No, sir, not I, I'm set this side,
I'll not let timber tip.

KNIGHT 2

More lifting, and less lip.

KNIGHT 1

LIFT UP!

(KNIGHTS 1, 3, 4, *lift the cross unsuccessfully.* KNIGHT 2 *hauls on the ropes.*)

KNIGHT 4

Let see!

KNIGHT 2

Oh, lift along!

KNIGHT 3

From all this harm he should him hide
If he were God.

KNIGHT 4
The Devil him hang!

KNIGHT 1
For great harm have I hent:
My shoulder is asunder.

KNIGHT 2
And shite I am near shent,
So long have I borne under.

KNIGHT 3
This cross and I in two must twin,
Else breaks my back asunder soon.

KNIGHT 4
Lay down again and leave your din;
(They lay the cross down.)
This deed for us will ne'er be done.

KNIGHT 1
Say, sirs, see if some engine
May help him up without delay
For here should workers worship win
And now go laik about all day.

KNIGHT 2
Workers worthier than we
You'll find 'em few enough.

KNIGHT 3
This bargain buggers me
I'm proper out of puff.

KNIGHT 4
So will of work never we were
I think this carl some craft has cast.

KNIGHT 2
My burden sat me wondrous sore;
Unto the hill I might not last.

KNIGHT 1

Lift up, and soon he shall be there;
Therefore fest on your fingers fast.

KNIGHT 3

Oh, lift!

(Music. Four KNIGHTS *lift cross, and carry it up the centre, and set it down.)*

KNIGHT 1

Heave ho!

KNIGHT 4

A little more.

KNIGHT 2

Hold then!

(Music ends.)

KNIGHT 1

How now?

KNIGHT 2

The worst is past.

KNIGHT 3

He weighs a wicked weight.

KNIGHT 2

So may we all four say,
Ere he was heaved on height,
And raised in this array.

KNIGHT 4

It made me bust my bollock stones
So boistous was he for to bear.

KNIGHT 1

Now raise him nimbly for the nonce
And set him by this mortice here;
And let him fall in all at once

146

For certes that pain shall have no peer.

KNIGHT 3

Heave up!

KNIGHT 4
Let down! So all his bones
Asunder now on all sides tear.

*(Music. KNIGHT 4 climbs up a ladder to the bridge above the stage.
KNIGHTS 2 and 3 throw up the ropes attached to the arms of the
cross, and KNIGHT 4 catches them. KNIGHTS 1, 2, 3 then heave
the cross into an upright position. KNIGHT 4 then grasps hold of
the head of the cross, and keeps it steady, while KNIGHTS 1, 2, 3
secure the cross in an upright position. KNIGHT 4 secures head of
cross against bridge and ties off the ropes on the rail of the bridge.)*

KNIGHT 1
(Looking over JESUS's limbs)
This falling was most fell.
T'cross cem down such a clout.
Now may a man well tell
Where t'Jew's least joints jut out.

KNIGHT 3
Methinketh this cross will not abide
Nor stand still in this mortice yet.

KNIGHT 4
Him as made mortice made it too wide,
That's why it waves. Young gormless get!

KNIGHT 1
It shall be set on ilka side,
So that it shall no further flit;
Good wedges shall we take this tide,
And fast the foot, then all is fit.

(KNIGHT 3 runs off stage to toolbags to fetch wedges.)

KNIGHT 3

Here are wedges arrayed
For that both great and small.

KNIGHT 1

Where are our hammers laid,
That we should work withal?

(KNIGHT 3 *drops wedges, and runs off stage again to fetch hammers from the toolbags. He finds them and holds them up.* KNIGHTS 1, 2, 4 *hold up their own hammers, laughing.*)

KNIGHT 4

We have them here, even at our hand.

(KNIGHT 3 *drops the hammers and moves back to the others on the stage.*)

KNIGHT 2

Give me this wedge; I shall it drive.

(KNIGHT 2 *hammers wedge into the base of the cross. Then* KNIGHTS *all move into the pit and look up at* JESUS.)

KNIGHT 1

(*To* JESUS)

Say, sir, how likes ye now
This work that we have wrought?

KNIGHT 4

(*To* JESUS)

We pray you, tell us how
You feel, or faint ye, what?

JESUS

All men that walk by way or street
Let this sore scene sink in thy soul.
Behold my head, my hands, my feet,
And brood ye deep on my dire dole.
If any mourning may be meet,
Or mischief measured unto mine.

148

My Father that all bales may beet,
Forgive these men that do me pine.
What they work wot they nought;

KNIGHT 1
(To crowd/audience)
Hey! Hark! He jangles like a jay.

KNIGHT 2
Methinks he patters like a pie.

KNIGHT 3
He has been doand so all day,
And made great moving of mercy.

KNIGHT 4
Is this the same that gan us say
That he was God's Son almighty?

KNIGHT 1
Therefore he feels full fell affray
And he is doomed this day to die.

KNIGHT 2
(To JESUS*)*
Vah! *'qui destruis templum . . .'*

KNIGHT 3
Or so he said he'd do.

KNIGHT 4
And sirs he said to some
He'd raise it up anew.

KNIGHT 1
To muster that he had no might
For all the craft that he could cast
All if he were in word so wight
For all his force now he is fast.
As Pilate doomed is done and dight;
Therefore I rede that we go rest.

KNIGHT 2

This race mun be rehearsèd right
Through the world both east and west.

KNIGHT 3

Yea, let him hang there still,
And make mows on the moon.

KNIGHT 4

Then may we wend at will.

(KNIGHTS 2, 3, 4 *begin to walk away.*)

KNIGHT 1

(*Picking up* JESUS'S *purple robe from the ground*)
Nay, good sirs, not so soon.
For certes us needs another note:
This kirtle would I of you crave.

KNIGHT 2

Nay, nay, sir, we will look by lot
Which of us four falls it to have.

KNIGHT 3

I rede we draw cut for this coat.

(KNIGHT 4 *gets three long nails and one shorter one from the toolbag, and holds them up in his fist to the others.*)

KNIGHT 3

Lo, see how soon all sides to save.

(*Each* KNIGHT *takes a nail.* KNIGHT 3, *thinking he has won, immediately picks up the robe to walk off with it, but* KNIGHT 4 *stops him and shows him a shorter nail.*)

KNIGHT 1

The short cut wins, that well ye wot
Whether it fall to knight or knave.

(*Meanwhile,* KNIGHT 1, *with his back turned to the others, has cut his nail with wire cutters so that his is the shortest.*)

KNIGHT 1

(Holds up his nail, and grabs the purple robe.)
    Brothers, ye need not brawl!
    This mantle is my gain.

KNIGHT 2

    The gaffer wins again.
    And we get bugger all.

(Exeunt KNIGHTS. *Song: 'The Moon Shines Bright'.)*

BAND

    The moon shines bright and the stars give a light,
    In a little while it will be day.
    Our Lord our God he calls upon us all,
    And he bids us awake and pray.

    So dear, so dear Christ loved us,
    And for our sins got slain,
    I'd have you to leave all your wicked, wicked ways,
    And turn to the Lord again.

    For the life of a man, it is but a span,
    And he flourishes like a flower,
    For he's here today, tomorrow he's gone,
    And he's dead all in an hour.

Christ on the Cross

Enter MARY MOTHER, MARY MAGDALENE, *and* MARY
SALOME *with* JOHN, *who stand before the cross.*
The three MARYS *kneel facing the audience.*
Enter CAYPHAS *and* ANNAS.
Enter PILATE.

PILATE

    See, seignors, and see what I say;
    Take tent to my talking entire.
    Avoid all this din here this day,
    And fall to my friendship all here.

Sir Pilate, a prince without peer
My name is full fitly to call,
And doomsman full worthy of fear
Of most gentle Jewry of all
      Am I.
Who makes oppression
Or does transgression,
By my discretion
Shall be doomed duly to die.
To die shall I doom them indeed,
Those rebels that rule them unright.

Thus loyally the law I unlap,
And punish them piteously.
But of Jesus I hold it ill hap
That he on yon hill hang so high,
      For guilt.
His blood to spill
Ye took him still;
Thus was your will,
With spitefullest speed was he spilt.

CAYPHAS
To spill him we spake in a speed,
For falsehood he followed i'fai';
With frauds all our folk gan he feed,
And laboured to learn them his lay.

ANNAS
Sir Pilate, of peace we you pray;
Our law was full like to be lorn.
He saved not our dear Sabbath day.
For that to escape were a scorn,
     By law.

PILATE
Sirs, before your sight
With all my might
I examined him right.

And no cause in him could I know.

ANNAS

Sir Pilate, your pleasure we pray;
Take tent to your talking this tide,
And wipe you yon writing away;
It is not best that it abide.
It suits you to set it aside,
And set that he said in his saw,
As he that was pricked up with pride,
'The Jews' King am I, comely to know,'
    Full plain.

PILATE

Quod scripsi, scripsi.
Yon same wrote I;
I bide thereby.

(*Exit* PILATE *followed by* CAYPHAS *and* ANNAS. MARY
MOTHER *with* MARY MAGDALENE, MARY SALOME *and* JOHN
begin to mourn for JESUS.)

ALL

Alas!

MARY MOTHER

For my sweet son I say,
Thus dolefully death thus is dight.

ALL

Alas!

MARY MOTHER

For full lovely thou lay
In my womb, this most wonderly wight.

ALL

Alas!

MARY MOTHER

That I should see this sight
Of my son so seemly to see.

ALL

Alas!

MARY MOTHER

That this blossom so bright
Untruly is tugged to this tree.

ALL

Alas!

MARY MOTHER

My lord, my life
With full grief
Hangs as a thief.

ALL

Alas!

MARY MOTHER

He did never trespass!

ALL

Alas!

MARY MOTHER

Son! Thou sorrowful sight!
Oh that me were closed in clay,
A sword of such sorrow me smite.
To death I were done this day.

ALL

Alas!

JESUS

Heloy! Heloy!
My God, my God full free,
Lama Sabatnye!
Wherefore forsook thou me?

(*Music. Exeunt* MARY MOTHER, MARY MAGDALENE, MARY
SALOME *and* JOHN.)

JESUS

Man on mould, be meek to me,
And have thy maker in thy mind,
And think how I have tholed for thee,
With peerless pains for to be pined.
The forward of my Father free
Have I fulfilled, as folk may find.
My friends that on me in faith relies
Now from their foes I shall defend,
And on the third day right uprise,
And so to heaven I shall ascend.
Then shall I come again,
To judge both good and ill,
To endless joy or pain;
Thus is my Father's will.

(Music. Enter a MINER, *the lamp on his helmet shining first in the face of* JESUS, *then, questioningly, on the faces of the audience.)*

MINER

What may these marvels signify
That here was showed so openly
    Unto our sight
This day on which that man did die
    That Jesus hight?
It is a misty thing to mean;
So strange a sight was never seen.
Our princes and our priest, I ween,
    Are sorely scared.
At baleful bodings that have been
    I stood and stared.
All elements, both old and young,
In their manners they made mourning.
    Creatures did cry
And kenned by countenance that their king
    Indeed did die.
The sun for woe he waxed all wan.
The moon and stars to blench began.

The clods did quake, and like a man
    Did make their moan
The stark stone and stiff stock
    Did grieve and groan.
Bodies like brocks out of burial burst.
Corses through t'earth's crust crept out and cursed.

To maintain truth is well worthy.
I tell you that I saw him die
And he was God's son almighty,
    That bleedeth ye before.
Yet say I so, and stand thereby
    For evermore.

But since ye set nought by my saw
    I'll wend my way.

(MINER *moves off the stage into the crowd/audience.*)

God grant you grace that you may know
    The truth some day.

(*Exit* MINER. *Song 'We Sing Allelujah'.*)

BAND
A man is like a rusty wheel
On a rusty cart.
He sings his song as he rattles along
And then he falls apart.

And we sing allelujah
At the turning of the year
And we work all day in the old-fashioned way
Till the shining star appears.

A man is like a bramble briar
Covers himself with thorns
He laughs like a clown when his fortunes are down
And his clothes are ragged and torn.

And we sing allelujah
At the turning of the year
And we work all day in the old-fashioned way
Till the shining star appears.

And a man is like his father
Wishes he'd never been born,
He longs for the time when the clock will chime,
And he's dead for evermore.

And we sing allelujah
At the turning of the year
And we work all day in the old-fashioned way
Till the shining star appears.

(Words and music: Richard Thompson.)

DOOMSDAY

CHARACTERS

JESUS
ADAM
EVE
ISAIAH
RIBALD
BEELZEBUB
SATAN
FOUR SOLDIERS
CAYPHAS
PILATE
ANNAS
MARY MOTHER
MARY MAGDALENE
MARY SALOME
ANGEL 1
LUCAS
CLEOPHAS
PETER
PAUL
JOHN
JACOB
WOMAN
TWO APOSTLES
THOMAS
TEN CITIZENS
JACOB 2
PHILIP
GOD (THE FATHER)
ANGEL GABRIEL
TWO WOMEN
ELEVEN BAD SOULS
ELEVEN GOOD SOULS
GOD (THE SON)
3 ANGELS
3 DEVILS

BAND

Look up, look up,
The lamb shall lead the way,
Look up, look up,
The dogs behowl the day.
And they shall bite,
Full bellied in their spite.
What care have they,
To take the lamb away.

Look up, look up.
The hand devides the gloom.
Look up, look up.
The prophet or the doom,
And should we die,
On whose word can we rely.
The truth to see,
Death or eternity.

Look up, look up,
The shepherd takes his place.
Look up, look up.
A mother hides her face.
And when we die,
Will there be friends to cry.
What hope have they,
Who turn their heads away.

Doomsday

The light from GOD's *miner's lamp illuminates the head of* JESUS.

JESUS

My Father me from bliss has send
To Earth for Mankind's sake.
Adam's miss for to amend
My death need must I take.

I dwelled there thirty years and two
Till hither hauled and hung on high,
In anger, pine and mickle woe
On cross this day to die.

Therefore to hell now will I fare
To claim back what is mine –
Adam, Eve, and others there
They shall no longer dwell in pine.

A light I will they have
To know I will come soon;
My body shall abide in t'grave
Till all this deed be done.

(The lights from various miner's lamps rake the darkness of limbo. The inhabitants of this limbo in hell have been there for 4,600 years. Profound gloom. Silence. Then the light from the miner's lamp (which illuminated Christ on the cross) rakes the gloom seeking for a way in. The light falls on the face of ADAM.*)*

ADAM

My brethren, hearken to me here.
This is the first hope we have had
In four thousand and six hundred year,
This glorious gleam to make us glad.
Wherefore I hope our help is near.
Now soon shall cease our sorrows sad.

(The light moves on through the darkness and discovers EVE, *who looks upon the face of her 'husband dear' for the first time in 4,600 years.)*

EVE

Adam, husband I love so,
This gleam that brings us glee
It is the light so long ago
In Paradise lit thee and me.

(The light moves on and discovers ISAIAH *who speaks to* ADAM *who clings close to* EVE.*)*

ISAIAH

Adam, through thy sin
Here were we put to dwell
This wicked place within;
The name of it is hell.
Adam, thou well understand
I am Isaiah who prophesied
That folk would in fell blackness bide
Until a light should them on land.
This light is all from Christ's command.
At his behest hath it hither hied.

(All round the still darkened stage the voices of the whole COMPANY *are heard, here and there, as to their fellows in hell, speaking of the light that has been seen shining through the gloom.)*

VOICES

This shining that us showers
And divides the darkness drear,
It is the hope that hath been ours
This four thousand and six hundred year.

This flame that on us flares
And dangs the dark in two
Comforts our carking cares.
This doom will God undo.

This lamp that on us lights
To this thought makes me tend:
This never-ending night's
Darkness and doom may end.

(The voices pass round the entire audience in all parts and then become louder so that they are heard by all, and gradually the individual voices blend into a unison saying:)

ALL

Come, Lord, come to hell anon!
Deliver us from darkness drear.

Four thousand six hundred years be gone
Since mankind first came here.

Come, Lord, come to hell anon!
Deliver us from darkness drear.
Four thousand six hundred years be gone
Since mankind first came here.

Come, Lord, come to hell anon.
Deliver us from darkness drear
Four thousand six hundred years be gone
Since mankind first came here.

(The sounds of this concerted murmured prayer, and outcry, alerts the DEVILS. *Sirens and alarms as* RIBALD *emerges from a sewer grate.)*

RIBALD

Since first that hell was made
And I was put therein,
Such sorrow never ere I had
Nor heard I such a din.
Help, Beelzebub, to bind these boys!
Such harrow was never ere heard in hell!

BEELZEBUB

Why roars thou so, Ribald? Thou roys!
What is betide? Can thou ought tell?

RIBALD

What? Hears thou not this ugly noise?
These that have lived in limbo long
They make moaning of many joys
And muster great mirth them among.

BEELZEBUB

Mirth? Nay, nay, that point is past.
More hope of health shall they never have.

RIBALD

They cry on Christ full fast
And says he shall them save.

BEELZEBUB

Ya, if he save them not, we shall.
For they are sparred in special space.
While I am prince and principal
Shall they never pass out of this place.
Say to Satan our sire
And bid him bring also
Lucifer lovely of lyre.

RIBALD

Already, lord, I go.

(Three loud knocks at the gates of hell. The voice of JESUS *is heard on the other side of the gates.)*

JESUS

Attollite portas principes
Open up ye princes of pains sere
Et elavamini eternales
Your endless gates that ye have here.

RIBALD

Out, harrow, out! What devil is he
That calls him king over us all?
Hark, Bellzebub!

(To other DEVILS*)*

And hasten ye
For hideously I heard him call.

BEELZEBUB

Way! Go spar our gates full fast with speed
And set forth watches on the wall,
And if he call or cry
To make us more debate
Lay on him hardily
And garre him gang his gate.

SATAN

Tell me what boys dare be so bold
For dread to make on us affray?

RIBALD

It is that Jew that Judas sold
For to be dead the other day.

SATAN

Ow! This tale in time is told,
This traitor traverses us alway.
He shall be here full hard in hold.
Look that he pass not I thee pray.

BEELZEBUB

Pass! Nay! He will not wend.
I wean he means to stay
And shapes him for to shend
All hell afore he hie away.

SATAN

Fie! Fie! Ye fools, thereof he shall fail.
For all his fare I him defy.
I know his tricks from top to tail.
He lives by gauds and guilery.
Thereby he brought forth from our bail
Of late Lazar of Betany.
Therefore I gave to the Jews counsel
That they should garre him die.

But I bid you be not abashed
But boldly make you boun
With tool that ye entrust
And ding the dastard down.

(They arm themselves with various weapons. Three loud knocks.
The voice of JESUS is heard again from the other side of the gates of
hell.)

JESUS

Principes, portas tollite
Undo your gates, ye princes of pride
Et introibit rex glorie
The king of bliss comes in this tide.

SATAN

Out! Harrow! What harlot is he
That says his kingdom shall be cried?

JESUS

Ye princes of hell, open your gate
And let my folk forth go.
The prince of peace shall enter thereat
Whether ye will or no.

RIBALD

What art thou that speaks us so?

JESUS

A king of bliss that hight Jesus.

RIBALD

Yea, fast I rede thou go
And meddle thee not with us.

BEELZEBUB

(To DEVILS)
Our gates will last I trust.
They seem so strong to me.

(Then louder to JESUS *over the wall)*
But if our bars shall bust
They shall not bust for thee!

JESUS

This stead shall be no longer stock.
Open up and let my people pass.

(There is an explosion.)

RIBALD

Out! Harrow! Our bail is brok
And busted all our bars of brass.
Tell Lucifer he's loosened t'lock.

BEELZEBUB

What is limbo lost, alas!
Harrow! Our gates begin to crack.
In sunder, I trow, they go.
All hell is lost, alas, alack!
Alas! I weep with woe.

SATAN

(From the back like all good generals)
I bade ye should be boun,
If he made mischief more,
To ding that dastard down
And set him both sad and sore.

BEELZEBUB

To set him sore that is soon said!
Come thou thyself and set him sore!
We may not bide his bitter braid.
He will us mar, though we were more.

SATAN

Fie, fainthearts, wherefore are ye afeared?
Have ye no force to flit him fro?
Look ye in haste to get me geared.
Myself shall to that gadling go.

*(SATAN is armed and equipped, and goes forth to meet JESUS.
SATAN seems threatening and formidable but JESUS defeats him
with a simple sign.)*

How, bel ami, abide
With all thy flaunt and fleer
And tell to me this tide
What mischief makes you here.

JESUS

I come to claim these kin of mine.
Them would I save, I thee now tell.
You had no power them to pine.
But for their good, forced guests of hell
Have they sojourned, not as thine
But in thy ward, as thou wot well.

SATAN

Ay, but where the devil hast thou been
This four thousand years or more?

JESUS

Now is the time certain.
My Father ordained before
That they should pass from pain
And dwell in mirth for evermore.

SATAN

Thy Father knew I well by sight.
He worked as wright his meat to win.
And Mary, methinks, thy mother hight.
They are all thou canst claim as kin.
So who made thee so mickle of might?

JESUS

Thou wicked fiend, let be thy din!
My Father dwells in heaven on height
With bliss that shall never blin
I am his own son
His forward to fulfil.
Together we are one
Or sunder when we will.

SATAN

God's son? Then should thou be full glad.
After no chattels need thou crave.
But thou hast lived ay like a lad
And in sorrow like a simple knave.

JESUS

That was for the heartly love I had
Unto man's soul it for to save,
And for to make thee mazed and mad
And for to goad thee from my grave.
My godhead I covered
In Mary, mother mine,
And ne'er was discovered
By such as thee and thine.

SATAN

Nay, bel ami, thou must be smit!

JESUS

(Calling on his ANGELS*)*

Michael, mine angel, make thee boun
And fast yon fiend that he not flit.
And, Devil, I command thee go down
Into thy cell where thou shall sit.

SATAN

Ow! Ay! Harrow! Help Mahoun!
Now wax I wode out of my wit.

(SATAN *falls into the sewer. Followed by* BEELZEBUB.)

I sink into hell's pit!

ADAM

Ah! Jesu lord, mickle is thy might
That makes thyself in this manner
Us for to help as thou hast hight,
When both forfeit I and my fere.
Here have we lived without all light
Four thousand and six hundred year.
Now I see this solemn sight
How thy mercy hath made us clear.

EVE

Blessed be thou, lord of life!
I am Eve, Adam's wife.

Thou hast suffered stroke and strife
For works that we have wrought.
Thy mild mercy hath all forgiven.
Death's dints on thee were driven.
Thy bright blood hath us bought.

ADAM

We thank this great goodness.
He fetched us from this place.
Make joy now, more or less.
All laud God for his grace.

JESUS

Adam and my friends in fere,
From all your foes come forth with me.
Ye shall be set in solace sere
Where ye shall never of sorrows see.

(*To* MICHAEL *and* ANGELS)

And Michael, mine angel clear,
Reserve these souls all unto thee
And lead them as I shall thee lere
To Paradise with play and plenty.

(*Procession off led by* ANGELS *with music.*
JESUS *is left alone.*)

My grave will I go till
Ready to rise upright
And so shall I fulfil
That I before have hight.

(JESUS *rises from limbo straight into his grave (a wooden wardrobe
with four doors) which is guarded by* FOUR SOLDIERS.)

SOLDIER 1

(*Bragging to audience*)

Lo, we say you for certain
We shall keep him with might and main.
There shall be no traitors with no train

171

Steal him us fro;
Such sawterell I swear be slain
And laid right low.

SOLDIER 2

Yea, certes, we are all ready boun.
We shall him keep to our renown.
On ilka side let us sit down
With all our gear
And soon we shall go crack his crown
Whoso comes here.

SOLDIER 1

Now may no one come here nigh
Whilst that I do watch this door.

SOLDIER 2

At this door so must I lie
And whoso come here, gets what for.

SOLDIER 3

And I shall tend this door this tide
Though there come here both Jack and Jill.

SOLDIER 4

And I shall keep the door this side
And whoso come here, shall I kill.

(The SOLDIERS *settle down in their various positions and almost
immediately start to nod: then spring sharply to attention as they
hear the approach of* CAYPHAS, ANNAS *and* PILATE.)

CAYPHAS

Hark, Sir Pilate, list to me
I shall thee tidings tell anew
Of one thing we must beware be
Or else hereafter we might it rue.

Thou wotest well how that Jesu
He said to us in words full plain,
He said that we should find it true

172

The third day he would rise again.
If these disciples come certain
And out of his grave steal him away
They will go preach and plainly say
That he is risen the third day.

PILATE
Now, gentle sirs, ye did vouchsafe
To go with me and seal the grave
That he arise not out of his grave
That is now dead.

We grant well let us now go
When it is sealed and watched also,
Then we be safe and without woe
And have of him no dread.

(They arrive at the tomb where the body of JESUS *is guarded by the* FOUR SOLDIERS. *The* FOUR SOLDIERS *close up the tomb.)*

ANNAS
Lo here is wax full ready dight.
Set on your seal anon full right.
Then ye be sure I now you plight
He shall not rise again.

PILATE
(Sealing the tomb with sealing wax and seal)
On this corner my seal shall sit
And with this wax I seal his pit.
Now dare I lay he shall never flit
Out of his grave certain.

ANNAS
Here is more wax full ready, lo!
All the corners ye seal also,
And with four locks lock it also
Then let us gang our way.
And let these knights abide thereby
And if these disciples come privily

To steal away this dead body
To us they bring them without delay.

PILATE

On every corner is set my seal
And now is my heart in wealth and weal.
Now may no sawterell away not steal
This body from under this stone.
Now, Sir Bishop, I pray to thee
And Annas also come with me.
Even together all we three
Homeward our way be gone.

(*Exeunt* CAYPHAS, ANNAS, PILATE *leaving the* FOUR
SOLDIERS *to take up their watch again, this time outside the sealed
tomb. The lights of two* ANGELS *make the soldiers sleep.*)

SOLDIER 1

My head dulleth.
My heart filleth
Of sleep.
Saint Mahownde
This burying ground
Thou keep.

(*He sleeps.*)

SOLDIER 2

I say the same
For any blame
I fall.
Mahownde's whelp
After thine help
I call.

(*He sleeps.*)

SOLDIER 3

I am heavy as lead
For any dread

I sleep.
Mahownde of might
This stone tonight
Thou keep.

(He sleeps.)

SOLDIER 4

By Mahownde, my God
I 'gin to nod
And sink.
Here I ask
To go to task
A wink.

(He sleeps.
Enter MARY MOTHER, MARY MAGDALENE *and* MARY
SALOME, *weeping and mourning, towards the tomb, round which
the* FOUR SOLDERS *are in deep sleep.)*

MARY MOTHER

Alas! To death would I be dight.
Never in the world was there woefuler wight.
My sorrow is all for that sight
    That I did see,
How Christ, my master, most of might
    Is dead from me!

MARY MAGDALENE

Alas! How stand I on my feet
When I think of his wounds all wet.
Jesus, that was of love so sweet
    And ne'er did ill,
With bitter blows they did him beat
    And for no cause him kill.

MARY SALOME

For no cause our foes each one
That lovely lord to death has done
And trespass he did never none

175

In no kind stead.
To whom now shall I make my moan
  Now he is dead?

MARY MOTHER

Now he is dead, my sisters dear,
Wend we will in mild manner
With our ointments fair and clear
  That we brought
To annoint his wounds all sere
  Our foes him wrought.

MARY MAGDALENE

Go we then, my sisters free,
For sore me longs his corse to see,
But wot I never how best may be
  Help have we none;
And who shall now here of us three
  Remove the stone?

MARY SALOME

That we do not though we were more
For it is huge and heavy also.

'MARY MOTHER

Sisters, we there no farther go
Nor make mourning,
I see two sit where we wend to
In white clothing.

(*Light from two* ANGELS's *torches breaks the chains around the tomb. Enter an* ANGEL *from the tomb.*)

ANGEL

Ye mourning women in our thought
Here in this place whom have ye sought?

MARY MOTHER

Jesus, that to death is brought.

ANGEL

He is not here the sooth to say,
The place is void that he in lay.
The cerements there see ye may
   That on him laid.
He is risen and went his way
   As he you said.
Even as he said, so done has he.
Through peerless power he rose up free.
He shall be found in Galilee
   In flesh and bone.
To his disciples wend now ye three
   And make this known.

MARY MOTHER

My sisters dear, since it is so
That he is risen death us fro,
This angel did us show
   Our lord so free,
Hence from here will I never go
   Before I him see.

MARY SALOME

Come let us wend away from here.
To Galilee now nigh us near.

MARY MAGDALENE

Not till I *see* that faithful fere,
   My lord and leech.
I say to you, my sisters dear,
   All this forth preach.

MARY SALOME

As we have seen, so we shall say.
Mary, our sister, have good day!

MARY MAGDALENE

Now very God, as he well may,
   Man most of might,

He wish you sisters well on your way
    And rule you right.

(Exeunt MARY MOTHER *and* MARY SALOME. MARY
MAGDALENE *is left alone but for the* SOLDIERS *still asleep.)*

Alas! Now nought hath any worth for me!
My caitiff heart will break in three
When I think of his body free
    How it was spilt.
Through feet and hands nailed was he
    And with no guilt.

I, who loved that sweet lad so
That bided ilka braid and blow
And graven is in t'grit below
    My bounteous boy!
Unless we meet, before I go,
    I'll ne'er know joy.

(Exit MARY.
Alarm clocks are rung by two ANGELS.
The FOUR SOLDIERS *wake with loud curses.)*

SOLDIER 1

What! Out! Alas! What shall I say?
Where is the corse that herein lay?

SOLDIER 2

What ails thee, man? Is he away
    That we should tent?

SOLDIER 1

Rise up and see!

SOLDIER 2
    Harrow, for ay!

SOLDIER 3

What devil is this that ails you two,
Such noise and cry and hullabaloo?
    Why, is he gone?

SOLDIER 4

Alas! Where is he that here lay?
Alas! Harrow! Devil! How got he away?

SOLDIER 3

Alas! What shall we do this day
That thus this warlock is went his way?
And safely, sirs, I dare well say
    He rose alone.

SOLDIER 2

When Sir Pilate wits of this affray
    We shall make moan.

SOLDIER 3

Can nought more then now be said?

SOLDIER 4

There is nought else but we be dead!

SOLDIER 2

When that he stirred out of this stead
    None could it ken.

SOLDIER 1

Alas! Hard hap on my head
    Among all men.

SOLDIER 3

For if Sir Pilate once doth wit
We were asleep when forth he flit
I tell you true we will forfeit
    All life and limb.

SOLDIER 4

Then fake we tales full ready fit
    To tell to him.

SOLDIER 3

Yea, that rede I well, so might I go.

SOLDIER 2

And I assent thereto also.

SOLDIER 4

Then shall I say a thousand foe
  With might and main
Came and took his corse us fro
  And us near slain.

SOLDIER 3

Methinks two thousand we should claim

SOLDIER 2

Nay, three thousand, four. In Mahowne's name!

SOLDIER 4

Five, six, seven thousand fierce foe came!

SOLDIER 3

Eight.

SOLDIER 2

Nine!

SOLDIER 4

Ten!

SOLDIER 3

Nay, less than fifteen does us shame.

ALL (*except* **SOLDIER 1**)

TWENTY thousand men!

SOLDIER 1

Nay, certes, I hold that not so good
As say the sooth even as it stood
How that he rose with main and mood
  And went his way.
To Sir Pilate, by Mahownde's blood,
  This dare I say.

SOLDIER 2

So will thou tell Sir Pilate until
These true tales of tidings ill.

SOLDIER 1

I tell thee true so that I will
    Straight in a trice.
And if Sir Pilate doth us kill
    No man dies twice!

SOLDIER 4

Wend we then to Sir Pilate's hall.
Cumbered cowards he shall us call
And we abide both braid and brawl
    Ere we are through.

SOLDIER 2

But still I shall to Sir Pilate all
    Tell full true.

(*Exeunt* FOUR SOLDIERS *to* PILATE'S *hall.*)

PILATE

Cumbered cowards I ye call!
Cumbered cowards I ye call.
Have ye let him go fro you all?

SOLDIER 3

Sir, there was none dare do but small
    When forth he fled.

SOLDIER 4

We were so feard down did we fall
    All dazed with dread.

PILATE

Fie! Fie upon your brag and boast
That of men your might was most.
In field and town and ilka coast,
    As each man knows.
Now all your worhip it is lorn

And ilka man may you now scorn
And bid you sit among the corn
   And scare the crows!

CAYPHAS

To say the best forsooth shall I
And bring profit to us all thereby.
Yon knights behooves them to deny
   How he did go,
And turn these tidings now awry
   So no man know.

ANNAS

Now, Sir Pilate, since it is so
That he is risen death us fro,
Command these knights to say, where'er they go,
   That he was ta'en
By twenty thousand of our foe
   And them near slain.

PILATE

(To SOLDIERS)

Now hearken what that ye shall say
To ilka men, by night and day,
That fifty thousand men in good array
   Came you until,
With force of arms bare him away
   Against your will.

Thus shall ye say in ilka land
And there cometh also with this command
A thousand pund each in your hand
   As your reward.
And friendship to you, understand,
   Shall I afford.

ANNAS

But look you say as we have kenned.

SOLDIER 1

Yes, sir, as Mahownde me mend,
In ilka country so ye us send
  By night and day,
Whereso we come, whereso we wend,
  Thus shall we say.

PILATE

The blessing of Mahownde go with ye
  By night and day.

(*Exeunt* FOUR SOLDIERS.)

PILATE

(*To audience*)
  Thus shall the sooth be bought and sold
  And treason shall for truth be told.

(*Song: 'What wondrous love is this?'*)

The Appearances

1. TO MARY

A GARDENER (JESUS) *works near the empty tomb.*
MARY *approaches him.*

MARY MAGDALENE

Tell me, gardener, I thee pray
If thou bare ought my lord away.
Say me the sooth. Say me not nay
  Where that he lies.
And I shall remove him, if I may,
  In some kind wise.

JESUS

Woman, why weepest thou? Be still!
Whom seeks thou? Say me thy will.
  Deny me not with nay.

183

MARY MAGDALENE

For my lord I look full ill,
The stead thou bare his body till
 Tell me I thee pray,
And I shall, if I may, his body bare with me,
Unto my ending day, the better I shall be.

JESUS

Woman, woman, turn thy thought!
Wit thou well I hid him not
 And bare him ne'er with me.
Go seek! Look if thou find him ought.

MARY MAGDALENE

In faith, I have him sought,
 But ne'er he will found be.

JESUS

Why what was he to thee
In soothfastness to say?

MARY MAGDALENE

Ah! He was so much to me
No long live I may.

JESUS

(Revealing himself)
 Mary, thou seeks thy god, and that am I.

MARY MAGDALENE

Rabony, my lord so dear,
Now I am whole that thou art here,
Suffer me to nigh thee near
 And kiss thy feet.
Might I do so, now and here,
 For thou art sweet.

JESUS

Nigh me not, my love, let be,
For to my Father, tell I thee,

184

Yet ascend I not.
Tell my brethren I shall be
Before them all in trinity
Whose will that I have wrought.

To my disciples say thou so
That meanwhile are all wapped in woe
That them succour I shall.
By name Peter thou call
And say that I shall be
Before him and them all
Myself in Galilee.

(JESUS *vanishes:*)

MARY MAGDALENE

To Galilee now will I fare
And his disciples catch from care.

2. The appearance to LUCAS and CLEOPHAS, pilgrims, on the
road to Emmaus

LUCAS

When I think on his passion
And on his mother how she did swoon
To die near am I boun.

CLEOPHAS

Such sorrow I saw her make
Under the cross when she fell down
For her son's sake.

LUCAS

Was never man in no kind stead
That suffered had so great misdeed
As he, to death before he sped,
Nor yet the care.

CLEOPHAS

His hurt is always in my head
Whereso'er I fare.

(Enter JESUS *also dressed as a pilgrim.)*

JESUS

Pilgrims, why moan ye so, I pray?
Why wend your way so full of rue?
Tell me, have ye missed your way?
I fain would know what ails you two.

CLEOPHAS

What way, for shame, man, didst thou wend
That thou wot not of this affray?
How could thou thus learn little, friend?
Annoy me now no more, I pray.

JESUS

I pray you, if it be your will,
These words you would rehearse me till.

LUCAS

Once thou wot what is come and gone
These past few days,
Methinks thou should make moan
And weep there in thy ways.

JESUS

Why, what is done, can ye me say
In this land this ilka day.
Is there fallen any affray
In this land somewhere.
If ye can, me tell, I pray,
Before I further fare.

CLEOPHAS

Ah! there they have slain a man for nought!
Jesus of Nazareth, full wise was he,
But bishops, cursed may they be!
Damned him and nailed him to a tree
That wrong never yet wrought.

JESUS

He shall rise up out of his pit
The holy prophets you tell so plain.
So turn your thought and change your wit
And trust well that Christ doth live again.

LUCAS

Live again? Man, hold thy peace!
How should a dead man ever rise.
I counsel thee such words to cease
For fear of Pilate and his spies.

CLEOPHAS

He was slain at a great assize
By council of lords all in a row.
Take care thou say not dead men rise
In every company where thou dost go.

JESUS

Why be ye slow to give your trust?
Did not Christ raise through his own might
Lazarus that dead lay under the dust
And stinked right foul, as I you plight?
To life Christ raised him from the pit
Again full right, that is certain.
Why can not Christ himself thus quit
And rise from death to live again?.

LUCAS

Ah Lord, give thee good grace
For greatly comforted me thou has
Go with us into this place
For here Emmaus Castle is.

CLEOPHAS

Now truly, sir, your words be good.
I have in you right great delight.
I pray you, sir, if that you would,
To dwell with us all this night.

JESUS

I must go hence anon full right,
For many messages I have to do.
I would abide if that I might
But at this time I must hence go.

LUCAS

Ye shall not go from us this night.
It waxes all dark. Gone is the day.
The sun is down; lorn is the light.
Ye shall not go from us away.

CLEOPHAS

This night from us ye go not away.
We shall you keep between us twain.

(They gently restrain him.)

To us, therefore, ye say not nay
But walk with us in't morn again.

JESUS

Since ye keep me might and main
With hearty will I shall abide.

LUCAS

Of your abiding we be full fain.
No man more welcome in this world wide.

CLEOPHAS

Now after your labour and far walking
Take this loaf and eat some bread
And then we shall have more talking
Of Christ our master that is now dead.

JESUS

Be ye merry and glad with heart full free,
For of Christ Jesu that was your friend
Ye shall have tidings of game and glee
Within a while afore ye wend.

*(*JESUS *breaks a loaf of bread as in The Last Supper.)*

> This bread that I do bless and break
> It is my corse, no common crust
> This beaker's t'blood shed for thy sake
> And sup of it ilk man you must.

(The PILGRIM *reveals himself as* JESUS *and then vanishes.)*

LUCAS

> Wemmow! Where is this man become
> Right here that sat betwixt us two?

CLEOPHAS

> He break the bread and laid us some.
> How might he hence now from us go
>   At his own list?

LUCAS

> It was our Lord I trow right so
>   And we not wist.

CLEOPHAS

> Rise, go we hence from this place
> To Jerusalem speed we apace.

LUCAS

> And tell our brethren all the case.

CLEOPHAS

> And say it thus:
> Our Lord alive in flesh and face
>   Appeared to us.

LUCAS

(Pointing to THE APOSTLES *and* WOMEN *singing while mending fishing nets and salting herring.)*

> Yea, here in this stead may we not stay
> Lo, hard on our heels draws nigh the next play.

WOMEN

Make haste! Make haste!

MEN

You'll be too late.

WOMEN

One fish, my dear.

MEN

I cannot wait.

ALL

For mi fine fry of herring,
Mi bonny silver herring.
Mind how you sell them
While the merry, merry bells do ring.

WOMEN

We've white and speckled bellied uns

MEN

We've white and speckled bellied uns

ALL

We've white and speckled bellied uns
While the merry, merry bells do ring.

WOMEN

Make haste! Make haste!

MEN

You'll be too late.

WOMEN

One fish, my dear.

MEN

I cannot wait.

ALL

For mi fine fry of herring
Mi bonny silver herring
Mind how you sell them
While the merry, merry bells do ring.

MARY MAGDALENE

(*To* PETER)

Hail, brother! And God be here!
News I bring to mend your cheer.
   Trust ye that it be true.
He is risen, the sooth to say.
I met him going by the way.
   He bade me tell it you.

PETER

Woman, with fables do not us now fret.
Some sprite it was that thou hast met
   Or it was nought!
We may trow on no kind wise
That dead men to life can rise;
   This then is our thought.

PAUL

The sooth is this: that for man's meed
Did Jesus, our brother, grimly bleed
   Through feet, hands and side.
With nails on t'rood they hung him long.
Wherefore, woman, thou says all wrong;
   The sooth is that he died.

MARY MAGDALENE

Are ye alleging I tell ye all lies,
That he that died on t'rood did arise?
   I with him spake, as I with you.
Therefore ye both, say I,
Put away your heresy,
   And trust my tale as true.

PAUL

But it is written in our law:
'There is no trust in woman's saw'
   No true faith to believe.
For with their quaintness and their guile

They can laugh and weep some while
   And yet nothing them grieve.

In our book there find we written,
(All manner of men well it witten)
   Of women on this wise:
Like an apple doth she seem
All aglow with gladsome gleam
   As there she lies,

But if a man assay a bite
It is full rotten, rotten right
   To the core within.
Wherefore in woman is no law
For she is without all awe
   As Christ me loose from sin.

(JESUS *appears with a great light.*)

JESUS

Peace and rest bide on thy brow.

(JESUS *vanishes.*)

PETER

Ah, brothers dear, what may we trow?
What was this sight that we saw now
   Shining so bright,
And vanished thus, we wot not how,
   Out of our sight.

JOHN

Out of our sight now is it sought.
It maketh us mad the light it brought.
What may it be?
            Certes, I wot nought.

JACOB

But certainly
It was but vanity in our thought,
   Nought else trow I it be.

192

(JESUS *appears again.*)

JESUS
Peace unto you evermore might be!
Dread you not, for I am he.

(JESUS *vanishes.*)

PETER
In God's name, *(crossing himself)* Benedicite!
  What may this mean?

JACOB
It is a sprite, forsooth, things me,
  That we have seen!

JOHN
A sprite it is, that trow I right
That thus appeared here to our sight.
It makes us mad of main and might
  So scared are we.
Yon is the same thing brought the light
  That we did see.

(JESUS *appears again.*)

JESUS
What thinks ye, madmen, in your thought?
What mourning in your hearts is brought?
I am Christ, so dread you nought.
  Here may ye see
That same body that has you bought
  Upon a tree.

For you these gates then have I gone.
Feel me firmly now ilka one
And see that I have flesh and bone.

(*The* APOSTLES *draw away.*)

Come, grope me now.

For flesh has ghost or spirit none
   That ye shall trow.

(No one comes forward, so JESUS *has to think of another way to demonstrate his physical existence.)*

To gar you ken and know me clear
I shall you show examples sere.
Bring now forth unto me here
   Some of your meat,
If ye among you, my brethren dear,
   Have ought to eat.

WOMAN

Thou loving lord that last shall ay,
Lo, here is meat that thou eat may,
A honey comb, the sooth to say,
   And roast fish too.
To eat thereof here we thee pray
  · If thou canst do!

(The APOSTLES *gather round as if trying to find out how a conjuring trick is done as* JESUS *eats fish and takes some honey.)*

JESUS

Now have I done, ye have seen how,
Boldly eating among you now.
Henceforth steadfastly in me trow!
   Such is my wish –

*(*JESUS *begins to disappear, then turns for a last word with* APOSTLES.*)*

And for all of you is left enow
   Of that fine fish!

*(*JESUS *disappears.)*

APOSTLE 1

Brethren, be we stable now of thought.
All wanhope put we away.
All misbelief now set at nought,

For we may safely say
He that mankind on rood hath bought,
From death rose the third day.
We saw the wounds in him were wrought
All bloody yet were they.

APOSTLE 2

Death that is so keen
Jesu overcome has.
As he told us, yet may we mean,
From death how he should pass.
All we apostles have him seen
Save only one: Thomas!

(Enter THOMAS *preoccupied with grief.)*

THOMAS

Alas for sight and sorrow sad,
Mourning makes me mazed and mad.
On ground now may I gang unglad . . .

PETER

Welcome, Thomas, where has thou been?
Now will thy sorrows cease, I wean.
Thomas! Our Lord! We have him seen!

THOMAS

Never shall I trow it true
That Jesus did to ye appear
Till my finger poke I through
The holes of nails and spear.

JACOB

Thomas, truly our Lord is live
That tholed the Jews his flesh to rive.
He let us see his wounds all five.

THOMAS

The wounds made by the spear and nails
To feel and find they are yet wet,

Then shall I trow in all your tales.
Till then no more me fret.

PAUL

Thomas, we *saw* his wounds all wet –
How he was nailed through hands and feet.
Honey and fish with us he ate.

THOMAS

(*Looking at the table*)
    The fish I see ye all have had
    And no morsel of it left for me
    Methinks mayhap was rank and bad
    And makes you ghosts and sprites to see.

ALL

Thomas! It is the truth we tell to thee!

THOMAS

What, leave, fellows, let be your fare!
Till that I see his body bare
And see my finger put in there
    Within his hide
And feel the wound the spear did shear
    Right in his side
Ere shall I trow your tales, I wean.

ALL

(*Angry and loud*)
    Thomas! those wounds have we all *seen!*

(JESUS *appears again.*)

JESUS

Peace! Brethren, unto you peace!
Let this unseemly strife now cease.
    And Thomas trow
As thou did ne'er trow nor trust me yet,
Thy finger put in my wounds wet –
    Yea, do it now!

(THOMAS *puts his finger in the wounds of* JESUS.)

THOMAS
(Kneeling)

> Mercy, Jesu, rue on me!
> My hand is bloody with thy blood.
> Mercy Jesu, I pray thee,
> Thy might that I not understood.

JESUS

> Thomas, for thou has seen this sight
> That I am risen as I thee hight
> Therefore thou trows . . .

(JESUS *turns to the audience.*)

> But ilka wight
>   Blessed be they ever
> That trows wholly in my rising right
>   Yet saw it never.

(*Exit* JESUS, *then from an upper level as the light of Pentecost shines on the* APOSTLES:)

> My sprite shall ever them inspire
> Through the force of heavenly fire.

THOMAS
(Singing)

> What wondrous love is this?
> Oh my soul,
> Oh my soul.
> What wondrous love is this?
> Oh my soul.
> What wondrous love is this?
> That calls the lord of bliss.
> To bear the dreadful curse,
> For my soul,
> For my soul,
> To bear the dreadful curse for my soul.

To God and to the Lamb,
I will sing,
I will sing.
To God and to the Lamb,
I will sing.
To God and to the Lamb,
Who is the great I am.
While millions join the theme
I will sing,
I will sing,
While millions join the theme I will sing.

(The APOSTLES *stand in a circle, praying. As they are praying they are surrounded by a hostile crowd of* SOLDIERS *and* CITIZENS.*)*

CITIZEN 1

Hark, misters, for Mahownde's pain
   How these mobbards mad are now.
Their master that our men have slain
   Has made them on his trifles trow.

CITIZEN 2

These lurdans say he lives again
   That matter may they never avow,
For as they heard his preaching plain
   He was away, they wist not how.

CITIZEN 3

They wist not where he went
   Therefore they shall fully fail,
But says them shall be sent
   Great help through his counsel.

CITIZEN 4

He might neither send cloth nor clout.
   He was never but a wretch alway.
But summon more men and make a shout
   So shall we best yon fools to flay.

CITIZEN 1

Here, fellows, here, come and take heed –
Yonder a drunken fellowship sits.

CITIZEN 5

Now, bid I, braid them with blows till they bleed!

CITIZEN 6

And hap on them heavily with hurts and with hits

CITIZEN 7

Now mar we their meeting and put them to pine!

CITIZEN 8

These apostles apraying are well wet with wine!

CITIZEN 9

(Himself drunk)
These dotterells, me seems, are drivelling with drink.

CITIZEN 10

With mickle meed are they mazed so I do think!

(The SOLDIERS *break up the meeting and fling* THE APOSTLES
aside.)

PETER

(Finally standing)
Sirs, alas, what do ye mean?
Why scorn ye now thus God's good grace?
It is no thing as ye do wean.
There is no drunk man in this place.
Wherefore right great is your trespass.

*(*PETER *lies on the ground and is then chained and dragged off.)*

But, sirs, list what it doth signify:
Fulfilled is now, to man's solace,
All God's gracious prophecy.

JACOB

From all foes Christ should us fend,

But thus in bale behooves us bide
Till the time his salve he send.
Our foes beset us on ilka side
That may we neither walk nor wend.

PETER

Full fearfully now do we fare
   For missing of our master Jesus.
Our hearts may not their burdens bear;
   Our foes do harm and hound us.

Us to betray and us to beat
   They are about both night and day.
For Jesus that we so seldom meet,
   As mazed men mourn we may.

JACOB 2

These folk that follow their faithless will
   And doomed our master to be dead,
With main and mood they would us spill
   If they wist how, in town or stead.

JOHN

Let us keep from all this carping keen
   And come but little in their sight.
Our master will come when we least wean.
   He will us rule and rede full right.

PETER

Of this carping now no more!
   It draws nigh the time of day.
At our meat I would we were.
   He'll send us succour as best may.

(*Enter* MARY MOTHER.)

MARY MOTHER

Succour soon he will you send
   If ye truly in him trow.

Your moan meekly will he amend,
　　My brethren dear, this may ye know.

The promise that he me plight
　　He has fulfilled, all that he said.
Deceived he never, day nor night,
　　Therefore, dear brethren, have no dread.

(JESUS *appears among them.*)

JESUS

Peter, and ye, my darlings dear,
　　As mazed men why stand ye there?
Wholly to you I have showed here
　　To bring your hearts from care.

Sent was I for your sake
　From my Father dear,
Flesh and blood to take
　　Of this maiden so clear.

Since to me ye sought
　　And wholly followed me
Of wonders that I wrought
　　Some have I let you see.

The blind as any stone, the dumb
　　I healed where I came by.
The dead I raised up from the tomb
　　Through my might from high.

And other works and wonders sere
　　I wrought wisely before you all.
My pain, my passion I told you clear
　　Wholly throughout as it should fall.

My rising on the third day
　　As ye by tokens many one have seen
Your trust had truly been away,
　　Had not my blessed mother been.

In her it rested all this tide.
    Your deeds you greatly ought to shame.
Here may ye see my wounds all wide
    How that I bought you out of blame.

(To JOHN*)*

But, John, think when I hung on rood
    That I betoke thee Mary mild;
Keep her still with stable mood.
    She is thy mother, thou her child.

Look thou love her, be her friend,
    And abide with her in well and woe,
For to my Father now will I wend
    There none of you ask whither I go.

PHILIP

Lord, if it be thy will,
    Shew us thy Father, we thee pray;
We have been with thee in good and ill
    And saw him never, night or day.

JESUS

Philip, that man that may see me
    He see my Father, full of might.
Trow thou not he dwells in me
    And I in him, if thou trows right.

In his house ye all shall dwell
    And thither now I wend away.
So ilka one here, fare ye well.
    My mother! My brethren! Have all good day.

(JESUS *begins to ascend on a fork-lift truck surrounded by a parachute towards heaven, and* GOD *in his fork-lift truck.)*

GOD

Ego sum alpha et omega
Vita, via, veritas
Primus et novssimus

202

JESUS

Father of Heaven, with good intent
   I pray thee hear me specially.
From Heaven to Earth thou me sent
   Thy name to preach and clarify.

Thy will have I done, all and some,
   In Earth will I no longer be.
Open the clouds, for now I come
   In joy and bliss to dwell with thee.

(JESUS *ascends to Heaven.*)

MARY MOTHER

So strange a sight now yonder is.
   Behold now, I you pray.
A cloud has born my bairn to bliss.
   My blessing bear he night and day.

But, son, think on thy mother dear,
   That thou hast left among thy foes!
Sweet son, let me not dwell here!
   Let me go with thee where thou goes.

Almighty God, how might this be?
   A cloud has born my bairn to bliss.
Now but that I know where he now is
   My heart would break, well wot I this.

His ascending up to bliss on high
   Is the source of all my joy.
My blessing, bairn, now on you nigh!
   And fend me, son, from foes' annoy!

My flesh it quakes like leaf on t'tree,
   To shake off showers sharper than thorn.
John! If thou be kind, I pray help me.
   My son missing makes me to mourn.

(MARY *falls.* JOHN *runs towards her and gathers her up in his arms
and takes her through the audience into her house.*

MARY *is sick. She sleeps in a wheelchair.)*

(The ANGEL GABRIEL *appears to* MARY.)

GABRIEL

(Very quietly at first in the presence of sickness)
Hail! mightful Mary, God's mother so mild!
Hail! be thou root of all rest, hail, be thou royal!
Hail! flower and fruit never faded or filed!
Hail! salve to all sinful; now say thee I shall:
Thy son to thy self me has sent
With this sign, and soothly he says,
No longer than these three days
Are left thee this life that is lent.

And therefore he bids thee look, that thou blithe be,
For to that bigly bliss thy boy will thee bring,
There to sit with himself, all solace to see,
And to be crowned his queen, and he himself king.
In mirth that ever shall be new,
He sends thee worthily, I wis,
This palm out of Paradise
In tokening that it shall be true.

(GABRIEL *throws a palm from Heaven, which* MARY *catches.)*

MARY MOTHER
For all his signs sere I thank seemly my son.
Unto him lastingly be ay loving
Such worship and worthiness me to have won
And to his bigly bliss my bones for to bring.
But, good sir, announce me your name!

GABRIEL
Gabriel! That before did bring
The bodeword of his bearing.
Forsooth, lady, I am the same.

MARY MOTHER

Now, Gabriel, that soothly is from my son sent,
I thank thee these tidings thou tells me until,
And loved be that lord for the loan me has lent,
And, dear son, I beseech thee,
Great God, thou grant me thy grace,
Thine apostles to have in this place
That they at my burying shall be.

GABRIEL

Now, fairest of face, most faithful and free,
Thine asking thy son has grant of his grace,
And says all same in sight ye shall see,
All his apostles appear in this place,
To work all thy will at thy wending.

(MARY *feels great pain.*)

And soon shall thy pain be past,
And thou to be in life that shall last
Evermore without any ending.

(*The* ANGEL GABRIEL *disappears. Enter* JOHN.)

JOHN

Mary, my mother, that mild is and meek
And chief of all chasteness, now tell me, what cheer?

MARY MOTHER

John, son, I wean I am woefully weak.
My sweet son, a sign have I had, an angel was here,
And doubtless he says I shall die.
Within three days, I wis,
I shall abide in bliss
And come to his own company.

JOHN

Ah! by thy leave, lady, announce me it nought,
Nor tell me no tidings that twin us in two!
For be thou, blessed bird, to thy bier brought,

Evermore while I wend in this world will I bewail you.
Therefore let it stand, and be still.

MARY MOTHER

Nay, John, son, my self now I see
At God's will must it needs be,
Therefore be it wrought at his will.

He brought me this palm from my son up there
Which I beseech as the angel me bad
That before my bier you shall it bear,
Saying my dirge, devoutly and sad.

John, son, of the priests have I heard it tell
How with foul plottings full fiendish and fell,
When my soul is past up to music and mirth,
Would they burn this body, it consume and quell.
For of this flesh Jesu whom they slew had his birth.
Therefore I beseech you, John, pray mark me well,
Help I be buried, and laid low in the earth.

JOHN

Ah! worthy, when thou art went, will me be full of
                                             woe!
But God give the apostles wist of thy wending.

(The APOSTLES *appear by miraculous means.*)

PETER

O God omnipotent, the giver of grace,
Benedicite dominus, a cloud now full clear
Umbelapped me in Judaea as I preached in that place
And I have mickle marvel how that I came here.

JACOB

Ah cease! Of this assembling can I not say
How and in what wise that we are here met,
For suddenly in sight here soon was I set.
Either mirth or of mourning mean well it may.

THOMAS

In diverse countries we preached of your son and his
bliss.
Diverse clouds each of us was suddenly covering.
We in one were brought before you now, I wis,
The cause why no man could tell of our coming.

JOHN

Fellows, my mother shall wend now, I wean,
Unto that bigly bliss her high bairn has us bought.
That we in her sight all same might be seen
Ere she dissever us fro, her son she besought.
And thus has he wrought at her will
When she should be brought on a bier
That we may be nighing her near
This time for to tend her until.

MARY MOTHER

My sickness it sits me full sare.
My maidens, take keep now on me!
And cast some water now on me.
I faint so feeble I fare.

(MARY *faints.*)

PETER

Brothers, each of you a candle taketh now right
And light them in haste while our mother doth dure
And busily let us watch in this virgin's sight
That when our lord cometh, all princely and pure,
He may find us waking, and ready with light.

(*The* APOSTLES *light candles. These should be the same as were
used for the Nativity. And as they watch over* MARY *the* WOMEN
sing 'Lay Me Low'.)

WOMAN 1

(*Atending* MARY)
Alas! for my lady so lovely of light,

My lady ay lastingly loved in the land!
O sore now it sears me to see such a sight!

WOMAN 2

Alas! Help! She dies in our hand.
Ah, Mary, of me have thou mind.
Some comfort us two for to find.
Thou knows we are come of thy kind.

MARY MOTHER

What ails you women, for woe thus wanly to weep?
Ye do me ding with your din, for me needs must die.
Ye should, when ye saw me so slip off to sleep
Have left off your lowing and let me lie.
John, son, gar them stop and be still!

(MARY *feels great pain.*)

Ah! that this pain were over past!
With good heart ye all that are here
Pray for me faithfully, my friends so dear,
For I must wend from you full fast.

Jesu, my blessed bairn, if thy will be,
I sadly beseech thee, my son, for my sake,
Men that are stead stiffly in storms or at sea
And are in will wisely my worship to wake
And then name me by name in that need,
Thou let them not perish nor spill.
Of this boon, my son, at thy will,
Thou grant me specially to speed.

Also, my blessed bairn, thou grant me my boon,
All that are in noy or in need and names me by name,
I pray thee, son, for my sake, thou succour them soon.
In all their showers that are sharp thou shield them
                                        from shame.

And women also in their childing
Now special thou them speed,

And if so be they die in that deed,
To thy bliss to abide them thou bring.

JESUS

(*Speaking from Heaven*)
Mary, my mother, come mildly to me.
After thee soon my servants will I send
And to sit with myself all solace to see,
In ay lasting life in liking to lend.

MARY MOTHER

I thank thee, my sweet son, I am woefully weak.
I may not now move me for mercy, almost,
To thee, son mine that made me, thy maiden so meek.
Here through thy grace, God's son, I give thee my
ghost.

(MARY *dies and her wheelchair is wheeled off by the* WOMEN.)

JOHN

Now, holy brother, Peter, I heartly you pray,
To bear this holy palm before this glorious body.
For ye be prince of apostles and head of our fay,
Therefore it seemeth you best to do this office truly.

(PETER *takes the holy palm.*)

PAUL

And I, Peter, with our brethren dear,
This blessed body shall help to the ground.
This holy corse now take we up here,
Sadly saying her dirge with devout sound.

JESUS

(*To* ANGELS *in Heaven*)
Mine angels, lovely of light, lighter than the leven,
Into the Earth wightly I will that ye wend
And bring me my mother to the highest of Heaven
With mirth and with melody her mood for to mend.

ANGEL

(To others)

> To bliss that bird for to bring
> Let us all now wightly be wending.
> This maiden's mirth to be mending
> A seemly song let us sing.

(A funeral procession, the APOSTLES *bear the coffin of* MARY *followed by* MOURNERS *singing a hymn.)*

APOSTLES and MOURNERS

> We're on our way to that fair land,
> Where the soul never dies.
> Where all this joy and peace and love,
> And the soul of man never dies.

> No sad farewell,
> There'll be no tear dimmed eyes.
> Where all is joy and peace and love,
> And the soul of man never dies.

(As the procession proceeds through the audience in the pit we see CAYPHAS, ANNAS *and* PILATE *on an upper level, as if poking their heads from a palace window.)*

CAYPHAS

> Hark, sir princes, what noise is all this?
> The earth and the air is full of melody
> I heard never ere, such a noise I now wis.
> Can ye ought say what they signify?

PILATE

> By Mahound, that most of mights is,
> I wot not what they be, but hugely they cry.
> I am afraid there will be something amiss.
> It is good privily among us we spy.

ANNAS

> Now I have lived this three score year
> But such noise I ne'er heard the like was of this.

My heart gins to shudder and quake all for fear.
There is some new sorrow springing, I wis.

CITIZEN

(*From street up to* CAYPHAS, ANNAS *and* PILATE)
Yea, that there is soothly, I say unto you.
The prophet's mother, Mary, is dead.
The apostles her burying pass here us through
And make all this mirth though we spit on their head.

CAYPHAS

Now that the caitiff queen is dead,
Ye rabble in row right rehearsed,
Fast harlots, I bid ye be speedily sped
And carry me back here that corse so accursed.

CITIZEN 1

To hassle these harlots me is full lief.
I shall snare those snivellers with right sharp showers.

ANNAS

Hence, in the Devil's name, and take me that thief
And bring me that beggar's body here to these towers.
And the disciples you slay.

CAYPHAS

Hie you hence, harlots, at once now I say!
Or the Devil's boys might break your bones.
Go stone me that body with your stones.
Out! Harrow! For Mahound! Wend on your way!

(*The hostile* CITIZENS *move to the procession. When they try to hit the* DISCIPLES *they are blocked by the* ANGELS *who make each would-be assailant strike himself.*)

CITIZEN 2

What the Devil does this mean?
I see right nought. Lo, I am blind!
My wits have wandered also, I wean.
I am full woe and mazed in mind.

CITIZEN 3

I am so feared I would fain flee.
The Devil him speed who here me brought.
I run, I rave, so woe is me.
Mad am I in mood and thought. .

CITIZEN 4

Some caitiff I can't see cracked open my crown
My manhood is marred! Oh mighty Mahound!

CITIZEN 5

Some shadowy shape right sharp has me shent
My body once buxom is broken and bent!

CITIZEN 1

Ah! Cowards, upon you now fie!
Are ye afeared of a dead body.
To that bier now boldly bound I.
All that company fear I right nought.

(He tries to push the coffin and his hands stick to it.)

Alas, my body is full of pain.
I am fastened sore to this bier.
Broken both my hands are twain.
O Peter! Now pray thy God for me here.

PETER

(Touching him with the palm)
Then honour this body that we now bear.

CITIZEN 1

Now, mercy God! And gramercy of this salvation.
In Jesu and his mother will I believe ere.

PETER

Take thou this holy palm and go to thy nation
And bid them believe in God if they will be pure.
Go now I bid thee the length of the land
And touch all the folk on head and on hand
And of their sickness shall they have cure.

(CITIZEN 1 *precedes the procession now, going among the* *audience touching some lightly on the head and the hand.*)

CITIZEN 1

Ye folk that languish in great infirmity
Believe in Christ Jesu and ye shall have health.
Through virtue of this holy palm that comes from the
                                                    trinity
Your sickness shall assuage and restore you to wealth.

(*He can repeat these lines as the procession proceeds towards the* *final resting place of* MARY. *The procession arrives at the grave* *where* MARY'S *body is to be put.*)

PETER

Now, holy brethren, this body let us take
And with all the worship we may lay it in the grave,
Touching it all at once; for her son's sake.
Honour the casket laid low in this cave.

(*All touch the coffin. Music. The* ANGEL'S *light strikes the coffin* *which bursts open revealing* MARY.)

ANGEL

Jesu, lord and Heaven's king,
Here is thy mother thou after sent.
We have her brought at thy bidding.
Take her to thee as thou hast meant.

MARY MOTHER

Jesu, my son, loved might thou be!
I thank thee heartly in my thought
That all this was ordained for me
And to this bliss thou has me brought.

JESUS

Hail be thou, Mary, maiden bright.
The time is past of all thy care.
Worship thee shall angels bright.
Annoy shall thou know never more.

MARY MOTHER

Jesu, my son, loved might thou be!
I thank thee heartly in my thought
That all this was ordained for me
And to this bliss thou has me brought.

JESUS

Come forth with me, my mother bright.
Into my bliss we shall ascend
As one in wealth, thou worthy wight,
And never more shall it have end.

Thou art my life and my liking,
My mother and maiden sheen.
Take this crown, my dear darling,
Where I am king, thou shalt be queen.

Mine angels bright, a song ye sing
In honour of my mother dear.
And I give you my blessing
Wholly, now and here.

*(Joyful music, as if the play were reaching a happy ending, then
suddenly with a dark chord* GOD *cuts it off for Doomsday to begin.)*

Doomsday

(GOD (THE FATHER) *appears as in a church.)*

GOD (THE FATHER)

First when I this world had wrought,
Wood and wind and waters wan,
And all kind of thing that now is ought,
Full well methought that I did then.
When they were made, good me them thought.
Then to my likeness made I man.
To sadden me man straightway sought,
Therefore me rues that I the world began.

When I had made man at my will
I gave him wits himself to wis
And Paradise I put him till,
And bade him hold it all as his.
But of the tree of good and ill,
I said: 'What time thou eats of this,
Man, thou speeds thyself to spill.
Thou art brought out of all thy bliss.'

Forthwith did man flout my forbidding!
He would have been a god thereby!
He would have knowledge of all known thing,
In world to have been as wise as I.
He ate the apple I bid should hang.
He was beguiled by glutton's greed.
Then him and all seed from him sprang
To pain I put for that dire deed.

Then long and late me thought it good
To catch those caitiffs out of care.
I sent my Son with full blithe mood
To earth, to salve them of their sore.
For ruth of them he rest on t'rood,
And bought them with his body bare.
For them he shed his true heart's blood.
What kindness may I do them more?

Then afterwards he harried hell
And took those wretches that were therein.
There fought that free with fiends full fell
For them there who were sunk in sin.
And then on earth he did go dwell.
Example he gave them Heaven to win.
In t'temple himself to teach and tell
To buy them bliss that may never blin.

Thus have they found me full of mercy,
Full of grace and forgiveness,
And they as wretches, utterly,

Have led their lives in licherness.
Oft have they grieved me grievously.
Thus have they quit me my kindness.
Therefore no longer, so say I,
Thole will I man's wickedness.

Men see the world but vanity
Yet will no man beware thereby.
Each day their mirror they will see
Yet think they not that they shall die.
All that ever I said should be
Is now fulfilled through prophecy.
Therefore now is it time for me
To make an end of man's folly.

I have tholed mankind many a year
In love and liking for to lend,
And scarcely find I far or near
A man that will his mood amend.
On earth I see sin everywhere.
Therefore mine angels will I send
To blow their brass, that all may hear
The time is come to make an end.

(*To* ANGELS)

Angels, blow your brass belive
Ilka creature for to call,
Clerk and clod, both man and wife,
Receive their doom this day they shall.
Each lad and lass that e'er had life
Be none forgotten, great or small.
There shall they see the wounds five
That my son suffered for them all.

(*Sterner*)

And sunder them before my sight!
All same in bliss shall they not be.
My blessèd bairns, as I have hight,
On my right hand I shall them see.

216

Then shall ilka wicked wight
On my left side for fearedness flee.
This day their dooms thus have I dight
To ilka man as he hath served me.

(Exit GOD (THE FATHER).*)*

ANGEL 1

Loved be thou, Lord of mights the most,
That angels made for messenger,
Thy will shall be fulfilled in haste,
That Heaven, earth, and hell shall hear.

Good and ill, each and every ghost
Fetch the flesh death rent, and rise,
For all this world is brought to waste.
Draw to your doom. Now near it nighs.
For I am sent from Heaven's king
To call you to this great assize.
Therefore rise up and give reckoning
· How ye him served in various wise.

(A prolonged blast, chilling and awful, from the ANGELS' *horns.
Here and there heads poke through the earth in a manner that
should deliberately remind us of the creation of* ADAM *and* EVE.*)*

BAD SOUL 1

Ah! Ah! Cleave asunder ye clods of clay!
Asunder break and let us pass!

BAD SOUL 2

Now may our song be welaway
That ever we sinned in deadly trespass.

BAD SOUL 3

Alas, I heard that horn
That calls us to the doom.

BAD SOUL 4

All that were ever born
Thither behooves them to come.

217

BAD SOUL 5
May neither land nor sea
Us from this doom hide.

BAD SOUL 6
For fear fain would I flee
But I must needs abide!

BAD SOUL 7
Alas, I am forlorn!
A spiteful blast here blaws.

BAD SOUL 8
I heard well by yon horn –
I wot whereto it draws.

BAD SOUL 9
I would I were unborn.
Alas that this day dawes!

BAD SOUL 10
Now must be damned this morn
My works, my deeds, my saws.

BAD SOUL 11
I never trowed this dreadful day
Would come to make us thus to moan.
Alas! Alas! What shall we say
When he sits on his throne?

(Now the GOOD SOULS *begin to push their heads through the clay.)*

GOOD SOUL 1 *(with* 2 *and* 3*)*
Loved be thou, lord, that is so sheen,
That on this manner made us rise,
Body and soul, together clean,
To come before the high assize.

GOOD SOUL 4 (*with* 5 *and* 6)
Of our ill deeds, lord, take no heed,
That we have wrought on wicked wise,
But grant us through thy grace indeed
That we may dwell in Paradise.

GOOD SOUL 7 (*with* 8 *and* 9)
Ah! lovèd be thou, lord of all,
That heaven and earth and all has wrought,
That with thine angels would us call
Out of our graves hither to be brought.

GOOD SOUL 10
Oft have we grieved thee, great and small,
But for that, lord, damn us not.

GOOD SOUL 11
Nor suffer us never to fiends to be thrall
That oft on earth with sin us sought.

BAD SOUL 1
Alas! Alas! that we were born
So may we sinful caitiffs say.

BAD SOUL 2
I hear well by this hideous horn
It draws full near to our Doomsday.

BAD SOUL 3
Alas, we wretches that are forlorn
That never yet served God to play.

BAD SOUL 4
Yea, oft we have his flesh forsworn.
Alas! Alas! and wellaway!

BAD SOUL 5
What shall we wretches do for dread
Or whither for feardness shall we flee?

BAD SOUL 6

We may bring forth not one good deed
Before him that our judge shall be.

BAD SOUL 7

To ask mercy is us no need
For well I wot that damned are we!

BAD SOUL 8

Alas, that we such life should lead
That dight us has this destiny.

BAD SOUL 9

As careworn caitiffs may we rise.
Sore may we wring our hands and weep.

BAD SOUL 10

For wickedness and woeful lies
Damned are we to hell full deep.

BAD SOUL 11

Wrought we never of God's service.
His commandments would we never keep.
But oft then made we sacrifice
To Satan, while all others sleep.

ANGEL

Stand not together. Part you in two.
All same ye shall not be in bliss.
My Father in Heaven has willed it so
For many of you have wrought amiss.

(*To* GOOD SOULS)

The good, on his right hand shall ye go.
The way to Heaven he will you wis.

(*To* BAD SOULS)

Ye wicked wights, ye flee him fro
On his left hand, as none of his.

(*Music. The end of the world is revealed.*)

GOD (THE SON)

This woeful world is brought to end.
My Father in Heaven he will it be.
Therefore to earth now will I wend
Myself to sit in majesty.
To deem my dooms I will descend;
This body will I bear with me –
How it was dight, man's miss to mend,
All mankind there shall it see.

Peter who by me bided ever near.
The dreadful doom this day is dight.
Both heaven and earth and hell shall hear
How I shall hold what I have hight.
And ye shall sit beside me here,
Beside myself to see that sight,
And for to doom folk far and near,
After their working, wrong or right.

APOSTLE 1

I love thee, Lord God Almighty,
Late and early, loud and still.
To do thy bidding bain am I.
I oblige me to do thy will
With all my might, as is worthy.

(PETER *sits at* JESUS's *right side*, MARY *at his left.*)

ANGEL 1

Believe, believe, and make your way
One and all before his throne.
Believe, believe, come is the day
To make you glad or make you groan.

ANGEL 2

Believe, believe, and make your way
Why do ye all still linger here?
Come is the day of wealth and woe
Go thither now your doom to hear.

GABRIEL

Believe, believe, why do you stay
When Doomsday's horn doth ye now call?
Come at last is Judgement day
Go, as I bade ye, one and all.

(Thee jaws of Hell open. Enter DEVILS.*)*

DEVIL 1

Fellers, array us for to fight!
And go we fast our fee to fang!
The dreadful doom this day is dight.
I dread me that we dwell too long.

DEVIL 2

We shall be seen ever in their sight
And warely wait, else work we wrong.
For if yon doomsman do us right
Full great a party with us shall gang.

DEVIL 3

He shall do right to foe and friend,
For now shall all the sooth be sought.
All wicked wights with us shall wend.
To endless pain they shall be brought.

(Music. A blast from the ANGELS' *horns.*
Hell mouth closes.)

GOD (THE SON)

Ilka creature now take tent
What bodeword I to you bring.
This woeful world away is went
And I am come as crownèd king.
My Father of Heaven, he has me sent
To deem your deeds and make ending.
Come is the day of judgement.
For sorrow shall all the sinful sing.

The day is come of caitiffness
All them to care that are unclean.
The day of bale and bitterness
Full long abiding has it been.
The day of dread to more and less
Of ire and trembling and of tene,
That ilka wight tha wicked is
May say 'Alas this day is seen!'

Here may ye see my wounds all wide,
The which I tholed for your misdeed,
Through heart and head, foot, hand and hide,
Not for my guilt but for your need.
Behold both body, back and side
So was I flayed that you be freed.
These bitter pains would I abide;
To buy you bliss thus would I bleed.

My body was scourged with scathe and skill;
As a thief full roughly was I threat.
On cross they hanged me on a hill,
Bloody and blue, as I was beat,
With crown of thorns thrusten full ill.
Thus spear unto my side was set.
Mine heart-blood spared they not for to spill.
Man, for thy love, would I not let.

Thus was I dight thy sorrow to slake.
Man thus behooved thee bought to be.
For torment no vengeance did I take.
My will it was for love of thee.
Man, sore ought thee for to quake,
This dreadful day this sight to see.
All this I suffered for thy sake.
Say, man, what suffered thou for me?

(*To* GOOD SOULS.)

My blessèd bairns on my right hand,
Your doom this day ye need not dread,
For all your comfort is command.
Your life in liking shall ye lead,
In this kingdom, this ay-lasting land,
That to you is due for your good deed.
Full blithe may ye be where ye stand,
For mickle in Heaven shall be your meed.

When I was hungry, ye me fed.
To slake my thirst your heart was free.
When I was clothless ye me clad.
Ye would no sorrow upon me see.
In hard prison when I was stead
Of my pains ye had pity.
Full sick when I was brought to bed
Kindly ye came to comfort me.

When I was weak and weariest
Ye harboured me full heartfully.
Full glad then were ye of your guest
And plained my poverty piteously.
Believe ye brought me of the best
And made my bed full easily,
Therefore in Heaven shall be your rest,
In joy and bliss to be me by.

GOOD SOUL 1
Lord, when had thou so mickle need,
Hungry or thirsty, how might it be?

GOOD SOUL 2
When was our heart free thee to feed?
In prison when might we thee see?

GOOD SOUL 3
When was thou sick or wanted weed?
To harbour thee when help did we?

GOOD SOUL 4

When had thou need of our good deed?
When did we all these deeds to thee?

GOD (THE SON)

My blessed bairns, I shall you say
What time these deeds were to me done:
When any that need had, night or day,
Asked you help and had it soon.
Your free hearts said them never nay,
Early or late, midday nor noon,
But as often as they did but pray,
Them need but bid to have their boon.

(Turning to BAD SOULS*)*

Ye cursed caitiffs of Cain's kin,
That never me comforted in my care,
Now I and ye for ever shall twin
In dole to dwell for evermore.
Your bitter bales shall never blin
That ye shall have when ye come there.
Thus are ye served for your sore sin,
For dire deeds ye have done ere.

When most need of meat and drink had I,
Caitiffs, ye catched me from your gate.
When ye were set as Sirs on high
And stood I outside, worn and wet,
You never brought me in to dry,
Pity to have on my poor state,
Therefore to hell you all shall hie.
Full worthy are ye of that fate!

When I was sick and sorriest
Ye visited me not, for I was poor.
In prison fast when I was fest
Then none of ye looked how I fore.
When I wist never where to rest

With dints ye drove me from your door.
But ever to pride then were ye pressed.
My flesh, my blood, oft ye forswore.

Clothless when I was oft, and cold,
Nearby to you did I bide naked,
House nor harbour, help nor hold,
Had I none of you, although I quaked.
My mischance saw ye manifold
But none of you my sorrow slaked,
But ever forsook me, young and old,
Therefore shall *ye* now be forsaked.

BAD SOUL 1
Lord, when had thou, that all thing has,
Hunger or thirst, since thou God is?

BAD SOUL 2
When was it thou in prison was?
When was thou naked or harbourless?

BAD SOUL 3
When was it we saw thee sick, alas?
When did we thee this unkindness?

BAD SOUL 4
When was it we let thee helpless pass?
When did we thee this wickedness?

GOD (THE SON)
When my bairns boons of ye bid
And needful asked ought in my name,
Ye heard them not, your ears ye hid;
No comfort from you caitiffs came.
Therefore fiends and fire ye fare amid;
Therefore ye bare this bitter blame.
To the least of mine when ye ought did
To me ye did the self and same.

(To GOOD SOULS)

My chosen childer, come to me,
With me to dwell now shall you wend.
There joy and bliss shall ever be.
Your life in liking ye shall lend.

(*The* GOOD SOULS *go to Heaven.*)

(*To* BAD SOULS)
Ye cursèd caitiffs, from me flee
In hell to dwell without an end.
There ye shall never but sorrow see
And sit by Satan the foul fiend.

(DEVILS *herd the* BAD SOULS *into the mouth of hell.
In the ensuing pause the audience should feel relief that the* DEVILS
have disappeared, and then suddenly the DEVILS *are among them.*)

DEVIL 1
I find here written on thy forehead
Thou were so stout and set in pride,
Thou wouldst not give a poor man bread
But from thy doors thou would him chide.

DEVIL 2
And in thy face here do I read
That if a thirsty man come any tide
For thirst though he should be nigh dead
Drink from him wouldst thou ever hide.
On covetousness was all thy thought.

DEVIL 3
In wrath thy neighbour to backbite
Them for to anger was thy delight.
Thou were ever ready then to endite.
On the sick man ruest thou nought.

DEVIL 1
Evermore on envy was all thy mind
Thou wouldst never visit no prisoner.

227

To all thy neighbours thou were unkind.
Thou wouldst never help a man in danger.

DEVIL 2

The sin of sloth thy soul shall shend.
Mass nor matins wouldst thou not hear.
To bury the dead man thou wouldst not wend
Therefore thou shalt to endless fire.
To sloth thou were full pressed.

DEVIL 3

Thou hadst rejoice in gluttony
In drunkenness and ribaldry.
Now the fires of hell draw nigh
And thou shalt know no rest.

DEVIL 1

And thou, slut, shalt thy ruin rue.

DEVIL 2

Thy life was one lecherous lay.

DEVIL 3

To all thy neighbours ye were a shrew.

DEVIL 1

All your pleasure was lecherous play.

DEVIL 2

God's men you loved but few.
Those in need ye never nursed.
Not even now a drop of dew
Shall quench thy everlasting thirst.

DEVIL 1

But, sirs, I you all tell,
If Doomsday had come much later,
Then we'd have to build our hell
grimmer . . .

DEVIL 2
grander . . .

DEVIL 3
greater!

(Exeunt DEVILS.*)*

GOD (THE FATHER)
Now is fulfilled all my forethought
For ended is all earthly thing.
All wordly wights that I have wrought
After their deeds have their dwelling.
They that would sin and ceased nought
Of sorrows sere now shall they sing.

GOD (THE SON)
But they that mended all their miss
Shall abide with me in endless bliss.

WOMAN
(Singing)
This aye neet
This aye neet
Every neet and all.
Fire and fleet and candle leet.
And Christ tak up thy soul.